MEET A BODY

An Improbable Adventure in
Three Acts

by Frank Launder and
Sidney Gilliat

SAMUEL FRENCH

Copyright © 1954 by Frank Launder and Sidney Gilliat
All Rights Reserved

MEET A BODY is fully protected under the copyright laws of the British Commonwealth, including Canada, the United States of America, and all other countries of the Copyright Union. All rights, including professional and amateur stage productions, recitation, lecturing, public reading, motion picture, radio broadcasting, television, online/digital production, and the rights of translation into foreign languages are strictly reserved.

ISBN 978-0-573-13263-6

concordtheatricals.co.uk
concordtheatricals.com

FOR AMATEUR PRODUCTION ENQUIRIES

UNITED KINGDOM AND WORLD
EXCLUDING NORTH AMERICA
licensing@concordtheatricals.co.uk
020-7054-7200

Each title is subject to availability from Concord Theatricals, depending upon country of performance.

CAUTION: Professional and amateur producers are hereby warned that *MEET A BODY* is subject to a licensing fee. The purchase, renting, lending or use of this book does not constitute a licence to perform this title(s), which licence must be obtained from the appropriate agent prior to any performance. Performance of this title(s) without a licence is a violation of copyright law and may subject the producer and/or presenter of such performances to penalties. Both amateurs and professionals considering a production are strongly advised to apply to the appropriate agent before starting rehearsals, advertising, or booking a theatre. A licensing fee must be paid whether the title is presented for charity or gain and whether or not admission is charged.

This work is published by Samuel French, an imprint of Concord Theatricals Ltd.

The Professional Rights in this play are controlled by Concord Theatricals, Aldwych House, 71-91 Aldwych, London, WC2B 4HN, UK .

No one shall make any changes in this title for the purpose of production. No part of this book may be reproduced, stored in a retrieval system, scanned, uploaded, or transmitted in any form, by any means, now known or yet to be invented, including mechanical, electronic, digital, photocopying, recording, videotaping, or otherwise, without the prior written permission of the publisher. No one shall share this title, or part of this title, to any social media or file hosting websites.

The moral right of Frank Launder and Sidney Gilliat to be identified as author of this work has been asserted in accordance with Section 77 of the Copyright, Designs and Patents Act 1988.

USE OF COPYRIGHTED MUSIC

A licence issued by Concord Theatricals to perform this play does not include permission to use the incidental music specified in this publication. In the United Kingdom: Where the place of performance is already licensed by the PERFORMING RIGHT SOCIETY (PRS) a return of the music used must be made to them. If the place of performance is not so licensed then application should be made to PRS for Music (www.prsformusic.com). A separate and additional licence from PHONOGRAPHIC PERFORMANCE LTD (www.ppluk.com) may be needed whenever commercial recordings are used. Outside the United Kingdom: Please contact the appropriate music licensing authority in your territory for the rights to any incidental music.

USE OF COPYRIGHTED THIRD-PARTY MATERIALS

Licensees are solely responsible for obtaining formal written permission from copyright owners to use copyrighted third-party materials (e.g., artworks, logos) in the performance of this play and are strongly cautioned to do so. If no such permission is obtained by the licensee, then the licensee must use only original materials that the licensee owns and controls. Licensees are solely responsible and liable for clearances of all third-party copyrighted materials, and shall indemnify the copyright owners of the play(s) and their licensing agent, Concord Theatricals Ltd., against any costs, expenses, losses and liabilities arising from the use of such copyrighted third-party materials by licensees.

IMPORTANT BILLING AND CREDIT REQUIREMENTS

If you have obtained performance rights to this title, please refer to your licensing agreement for important billing and credit requirements.

MEET A BODY

Presented by Laurence Olivier Productions Ltd at the Duke of York's Theatre, London, on the 21st July 1954, with the following cast of characters:

(in the order of their appearance)

REGINALD WILLOUGHBY-PRATT, a B.B.C. announcer	*William Kendall*
MONTAGUE	*Patrick Cargill*
WILLIAM BLAKE, a vacuum-cleaner salesman	*Brian Reece*
ANN VINCENT, Reginald's fiancée	*Joy Shelton*
MR HAWKINS	*Duncan Lewis*
POLICE SERGEANT BASSET	*Noel Coleman*
WINIFRED	*Christine Pollon*
CHARLES BOUGHTFLOWER	*Cyril Chamberlain*
THE LANDLORD, of the *Green Man*	*Julian Mitchell*
LILY, the barmaid	*Barbara Leigh*
SIR GREGORY UPSHOTT	*Lloyd Pearson*
JOAN WOOD	*Dorothy Gordon*

The play directed by HENRY KENDALL
The settings designed by HAL HENSHAW

SYNOPSIS OF SCENES

PROLOGUE
A B.B.C. Studio

ACT I
The lounge of a small house in St John's Wood.
Early evening in May

ACT II
SCENE 1 The lounge of the house next door.
Immediately following
SCENE 2 The same as Act I. The same evening

ACT III
The Bar Parlour of the *Green Man*, Newcliffe.
The same night

Time—the present

PROLOGUE

Scene—*A B.B.C. studio.*

The light from a small spot in the footlights is focused on a cameo set c, *in front of* Running Tabs. *There is a table and chair and a waste-paper basket. On the table is set a desk lamp, a microphone and some sheets of typescript.*

When the Curtain *rises,* Reginald Willoughby-Pratt, *a B.B.C. announcer, is seated at the table, reading the news into the microphone. His one really distinctive feature is a moustache which, in the modern fashion, inclines towards the fully-fledged, but stops halfway before it can interfere seriously with his vocation.*

Reginald (*reading*) ". . . and depended, he said, on the decision of the new French Government, if—and when—it was formed. (*He pauses*) At a luncheon in the City today, Sir Gregory Upshott, the recently appointed Special Envoy to the Middle East, told the guests of his high hopes for his forthcoming mission. The Government had appealed to him to come out of retirement and put to use once again his lifelong experience of peoples, personalities and conditions in the Middle East." (*He turns away from the microphone to indulge in a slight fit of coughing, then leans towards the microphone. Apologetically*) I beg your pardon. (*He reads*) "His object was to persuade the countries in that vital strategic area that it was either a question of hanging together or hanging separately. Certain minority elements there had threatened to take any steps, however extreme, that might be necessary to defeat the object of his mission. Sir Gregory said that he remained quite unintimate, and . . ." (*He breaks off, studies his script for a moment then leans towards the microphone*) I'll read that again. (*He reads*) "Sir Gregory said that he remained quite *unintimidated,* and concluded by remarking that it was a platitude, but a true one, to say that in the common interest we must all unite. The moment of impact might not be far ahead, and if he could help to achieve a completely new outlook, then his task would be done, and he would be able to retire, this time finally, from the public scene." (*He leans towards the microphone. Intimately*) A recording of Sir Gregory's speech will be broadcast in the Home Service at ten forty-five this evening. (*He reads*) "At question time in the house today, the Prime Minister denied that the cuts in the Army, Navy and Air Force estimates had anything to do with the Government's entry into the film business."

Reginald's *voice fades as the spotlight dims quickly to* Black-Out *and—*

the Curtain *quickly falls*

ACT I

SCENE—*The lounge of a small house in St John's Wood. Early evening in May.*

It is a small, newly built house of modern design, as the Estate Agent terms it, "a veritable suntrap". The front door is facing the audience in an arched alcove up C. *A door across the corner up* R *leads to a passage and thence to the kitchen. The fireplace is* R, *and there is a large casement window* L *with a built-in seat overlooking the road and the houses opposite. The staircase to the bedrooms is through an arch up* RC *and runs up and off* R. *There is a small cupboard built into the* L *wall of the front door alcove. When the front door is open there is a view of a small front garden, the road and the houses opposite. The furniture is modern, almost painfully brand new and is covered with dust sheets. The floor is carpeted and there is a new rust-coloured Indian rug in front of the fireplace. There is a certain tentativeness in the arrangement of the furniture, an impression reinforced by the presence of a packing-case full of books and a pile of pictures on the floor down* L. *The main pieces of furniture are a grand piano and stool* L, *an easy chair, a circular table* LC *with a upright chair above it, a sofa* RC *and an occasional table up* RC. *A telephone receiver on the window seat is concealed by the upstage window curtain.*

(See the Ground Plan and Photograph of the scene)

When the CURTAIN *rises, it is six-thirty in the evening. The stage is empty, the window curtains are closed and the light is dim except for a bright light streaming through the open door* R. *The room shows evidence of a slight disturbance. The corner of a rug below the table* LC *is turned back, the chair up* LC *is overturned on its side and one of the sofa cushions is on the floor. A man's jacket and bowler hat are on the table* LC *and there is a bottle of whisky, a syphon of soda and some glasses on the table* RC. *After a moment,* MONTAGUE *enters* R. *He is a dark, compact little man, of whom it is possibly sufficient to say that he has the look of a rather intense shop steward. He is in his shirt sleeves, with the cuffs turned back, and he is wiping his hands on a towel. He is breathing fast and altogether his manner suggests that he has just suffered a considerable shock to his nervous system and is anxious to clear out of the house as soon as possible. In the distance, a church clock strikes the half hour.* MONTAGUE *hurriedly picks up the cushion, sets the chair on its legs and kicks the rug with his foot to straighten it. He tosses the towel on to the table* LC, *picks up his jacket, puts it on then crosses to the window and opens the curtains. He turns from the window and in the brighter light catches sight of a stain on the carpet above the easy chair* LC. *Muttering, he grabs the towel, bends down and vigorously*

To face page 2:—Meet A Body *Photograph by Houston Rogers*

rubs the stain with the towel. *Under cover of the chair he substitutes the towel for one stained with red previously concealed under the chair. He rises, tosses the towel on to the table* LC, *steps back, studies his work, then grabs his hat, moves to the front door, opens it, takes a last look around, and realizes he has left the stained towel in view. He pushes the door to, but does not latch it, hurriedly gathers up the towel and stuffs it into his pocket. As he does so, he sees the whisky on the table* LC. *He hesitates, crosses, picks up the bottle, pours a drink into a glass and swallows it down with a gulp. As he drinks, the front door is slowly pushed open and* WILLIAM BLAKE *peers in. He is a young vacuum-cleaner salesman and carries a wooden case containing his demonstration model.*

WILLIAM. Anybody at home? (*He comes into the room and puts his case on the floor* L *of the doorway*)

(MONTAGUE *gasps and swivels round*)

(*He sees Montague*) Ah, good evening.
MONTAGUE (*putting the glass on the table*) What—what is it?
WILLIAM (*moving to* L *of Montague*) I have an appointment with Mrs Bostock.
MONTAGUE. Mrs—Bostock?
WILLIAM. That's it. "Windyridge", Hilcot Road, St John's Wood—correct, I think?
MONTAGUE. What? (*His face clears as if this has given him the answer to the problem*) Yes. Of course. That's right. "Windyridge."
WILLIAM. Splendid. (*He promptly closes the front door*)
MONTAGUE (*quickly*) She's out.
WILLIAM. What?
MONTAGUE. Mrs Bostock's out. (*He crosses to the door* R)
WILLIAM. But she asked me to call at six-thirty.
MONTAGUE. She must have overlooked it—that's it—she'll have forgotten. (*He gains confidence*) She went out at about six, said she was going to the pictures.
WILLIAM. Ah, well! One can't compete with Gregory Peck. (*He opens his case and takes out the rubber tube*)
MONTAGUE (*suddenly apprehensive*) Did you ring the bell?
WILLIAM (*shaking his head; smilingly*) I'm sorry if I came in un-heralded, so to speak, but the door was open, and in my job a foot in the door is worth two on the step. You see, I represent the Little Wizard of the Carpet.
MONTAGUE. The what?
WILLIAM (*taking a business card from his pocket*) I telephoned Mrs Bostock and arranged the demonstration. (*He hands the card to Montague*) My card.

(MONTAGUE *looks at the card and reacts with some relief*)

MONTAGUE. Oh, I see. You're a vacuum cleaner.

WILLIAM. Well, not incarnate, sir. Just the human agency. (*He takes the card from Montague*) Pardon me—it's the only one I've got. (*He puts the card in his pocket*)

MONTAGUE (*with a step towards the front door*) I'll tell Mrs Bostock you called. Sorry you've wasted a visit—how about the same time tomorrow?

WILLIAM (*keeping between Montague and the front door*) Please don't bother to apologize, Mr Bostock.

MONTAGUE. Eh?

WILLIAM. It is Mr Bostock, I take it?

MONTAGUE. Yes, yes. Of course.

WILLIAM. Good. Good. Then I couldn't have hoped for a happier accident.

MONTAGUE (*hastily*) I'm sorry but I'm afraid I'm very busy just now.

WILLIAM. This is the very machine for the busy man. (*He attempts to remove the body of the cleaner from the case*) The whole thing assembles in twenty-five seconds. (*The cleaner jams in the case and he tugs at it*) If I can get it out.

MONTAGUE. I haven't the time to wait while . . .

WILLIAM (*extracting the cleaner from the case*) May I just explain? (*He puts the cleaner on the floor*) The ordinary cleaner sweeps as it cleans, the superior cleaner beats as it sweeps as it cleans—but the Electro-Broom, the Little Wizard of the Carpet, *disinfects* as it beats as it sweeps as it cleans—thanks to our own inbuilt germicidal deodorant. Have you any idea what that carpet hides, sir? Millions of tiny germs. I won't go into what they're doing, but if they're allowed to increase in numbers, what do you think will happen?

MONTAGUE. I've no idea, but . . .

WILLIAM. Now, we have some rather cunning gadgets here, sir. (*He takes an attachment from the case*) This is for getting into small places and cleaning gentlemen's hats—(*he exchanges the attachment for another*) this is for slightly bigger places and—(*he runs the attachment over Montague's suit*) cleaning gentlemen's suits—(*he exchanges the attachment for another*) this is for larger places and carpets and so on—(*he exchanges the attachment for another*) and this . . . (*He breaks off and looks puzzled*) Excuse me, sir. (*He takes the instruction pamphlet from the case and studies it*) Oh, yes—(*he laughs*) how silly of me. (*He replaces the attachment in the case*)

MONTAGUE. I'm sure Mrs Bostock will be very interested—tomorrow.

WILLIAM. While I'm assembling it, you might care to glance at this folder giving five unreasonable answers—I mean unanswerable reasons why you should choose our machine in preference to any other.

MONTAGUE. I've said I'm not interested.

WILLIAM. But surely, sir, when it comes to a question of how your money's spent, you must be interested, if only morbidly.

MONTAGUE. I tell you I'm not interested in spending it on a vacuum cleaner. (*He crosses nervously below William and the table* LC *to the window*)

WILLIAM (*putting the pamphlet in the case*) I beg your pardon, sir, but I think you said you were willing to let Mrs Bostock see it tomorrow.

MONTAGUE. It doesn't matter what I said.

WILLIAM. I'm only too afraid you're right. Once she sets eyes on it—you are—forgive the expression—a dead duck.

MONTAGUE. Will you pack that thing up and go!

WILLIAM. At times like this I ask myself what would be the point of having learnt how to overcome sales resistance if there were no sales resistance to overcome.

(MONTAGUE *glances uneasily out of the window*)

Expecting somebody?

MONTAGUE. No. (*He looks at William in despair and gives the whole thing up*) How long will you be?

WILLIAM. The Electro-Broom is noted for its extreme ease and rapidity of assembly—(*he picks up the cleaner and struggles to fit the rubber tube to it*) in fact it almost assembles itself—when—you—understand—it. (*He fails to fit the tube*) I've only been at this a week. (*He hands the body of the machine to Montague*) Look, sir, would you mind giving me a hand with this? It's a perfect devil until you get used to it. (*He connects the tube*) You see, the whole thing fits together.

(*The tube falls out*)

Oh. . . .

MONTAGUE (*looking uneasily at William*) I've got something to sort out. (*He puts the cleaner on the table* LC) In the next room. (*He crosses to* R) I won't be a minute.

WILLIAM. Fine.

(MONTAGUE *exits* R)

(*He assembles the cleaner*) I'm glad I persuaded you. Seriously, this isn't a bad little machine at all—if you know anything about it. (*He stands the assembled machine on the floor beside the case*) Right, that's fixed it. (*He calls*) Can you hear me, Mr Bostock?

MONTAGUE (*off; calling*) Yes. All right.

WILLIAM (*shouting*) I'm going to put down a layer of soot and one of sand. (*He takes two small bags from his case and crosses to the fireplace*) Yes, the same old routine. Rather corny, you might say, but I can't persuade the firm to change it. (*He empties the contents of the bags on to the hearthrug*) I'm putting it on the hearth here. No need to worry—ten seconds and it's in the bag. (*He laughs, crosses to* C, *drops the empty bags into the case and picks up the lead and plug*) Now all we've got to do is plug it in. Where's the point? (*He wanders about the room looking for the point which he locates in the skirting board above the fireplace*) Ah, there it is. (*He plugs in the lead*) This reminds me of a rather dim colleague of mine. He smothered a new carpet with soot and then actually found there was no electricity laid on. He took a poor view of it when we laughed ourselves silly, but . . . (*He switches on the plug then crosses and clicks over the switch on the cleaner itself. Nothing happens. He repeats the action. Still nothing happens. He bends down and examines the plug, then crosses to the front door and clicks on the light switch in the alcove. The lights do not come on. Crestfallen, he surveys the mess on the hearthrug and looks apprehensively towards the kitchen*) Oh—(*he calls*) Mr Bostock.

(*There is no reply*)

(*He moves to the door* R) You remember that silly fellow I was telling you about? Mr Bostock, have you got a minute.

(WILLIAM *exits* R)

(*As he goes*) Why didn't you tell me there was no electricity?

(*There is a slight pause*)

(*Off*) Mr Bostock! Where are you?

(WILLIAM *re-enters* R, *looking extremely puzzled, and carrying Montague's bowler hat which he dubiously examines and lays on the back of the sofa*)

(*He goes to the foot of the stairs and calls*) Mr Bostock.

(WILLIAM *exits up the stairs*)

(*As he goes*) Mr Bostock!

(*There is a slight pause*)

(*Off*) Hello, there!

(WILLIAM *re-enters down the stairs*)

That's funny. (*He crosses towards the window. As he does so, he notices the mark on the carpet* LC, *pauses to give it a curious look, then bends down and dabs his finger on it. He lifts his finger up, looks at it, and whistles. He runs his hand up the leg of the piano and stands up with a cry of alarm, wiping blood off his fingers. He glances nervously around the room, cautiously lifts the dust sheet on the table* LC, *and peers underneath. Finding nothing, he makes for the front door and pulls up as he spots a cupboard in the left wall of the alcove. He goes to the cupboard door, hesitates, and then summoning up his courage, jerks open the door. A mop falls out. He gives a shout, pushes it back, closes the door and retires hurriedly to the sofa. This gives him an idea and he cautiously looks under the dust sheet and prods the cushions. Then he bends down, peers under the sofa, and pulls out a lady's umbrella from under it. Going down more or less flat, he searches underneath the sofa and reaches as far as he can stretch, feeling with his hand)*

(ANN VINCENT *lets herself in by the front door. She wears outdoor clothes and carries her handbag, a parcel and a modiste's box. She takes her key out of the lock, puts it in her bag, closes the door, and puts her bag and parcels on the window seat. She then turns, crosses to* C *and sees William grovelling by the sofa.* ANN *screams.* WILLIAM, *startled, looks up)*

ANN. Who are you? What are you doing here?
WILLIAM. Oh—good evening.
ANN. What are you doing down there?
WILLIAM (*waving the umbrella*) Rescuing an umbrella.
ANN. Who are you?
WILLIAM (*getting to his feet*) I represent the Little Wizard of the Carpet, madam.
ANN. What?
WILLIAM. You asked me to call at six-thirty—remember? (*He puts the umbrella on the sofa*)
ANN. I did?
WILLIAM. That's right. You are Mrs Bostock, I take it?
ANN. No.
WILLIAM. No?
ANN. No.
WILLIAM. Oh. Then, of course, you wouldn't know. I made an appointment with Mrs Bostock.
ANN. Who is Mrs Bostock?
WILLIAM. Don't you know?
ANN. I've never heard of her in my life.
WILLIAM. But she asked me to call here and demonstrate a vacuum cleaner.
ANN (*coldly*) I'm afraid you've come to the wrong house.
WILLIAM. Oh, no. I took down the address.
ANN. Which house did you want?
WILLIAM. "Windyridge".
ANN. Well, this is "Appleby". (*She takes off her hat and puts it on the window seat*)
WILLIAM. Oh, I see what's happened. *You've* come to the wrong house.
ANN. Don't be absurd. You think I don't know my own house when I see it?
WILLIAM. Your house?
ANN. Yes.
WILLIAM. Are you sure?
ANN (*removing her coat*) Of course I'm sure. I told you, I live here myself—at least, I'll start doing so next month. (*She puts her coat on the window seat*)

WILLIAM. I can see how it happened. All the houses on this side of the road are exactly alike.

ANN. Do you think I don't know my own furniture when I see it? (*She crosses to the fireplace*) I got that table at Heal's—it only came yesterday—*and* the curtains, *and* the sofa, *and* the ... (*She sees the soot and sand on the hearthrug and turns furiously to William*) Oh! Are you responsible for this?

WILLIAM. Only indirectly. You see, I was giving a demonstration and Mr Bostock omitted to tell me there was no electricity laid on.

ANN. You've ruined my hearthrug.

WILLIAM. Are you sure it's your rug?

ANN. Of course I am. I tell you, this is "Appleby".

WILLIAM. I'm awfully sorry—"Windyridge".

ANN. Have you been drinking?

WILLIAM. I regret to say—no.

ANN (*controlling herself with difficulty*) Well, it's easily settled. (*She crosses to the front door*) The name's hanging over the door.

WILLIAM. Yes. I noticed it when I came in.

ANN. Exactly—"Appleby".

WILLIAM. "Windy-"—allow me. (*He crosses to the front door, opens it and stretches up on the threshold to reach over the top of the porch outside*) Apart from the fact that the customer is always right, I very much dislike having to prove a lady wrong, especially on so short an acquaintance, but I think you'll have to agree with me once and for all, the name is definitely—(*he brings down into view one of those detachable house name-plates which are suspended by a wire for unhooking, with the name in gold letters. He breaks off as he looks at the name-plate, which has "Appleby" on it*) "Wind—elby".

(ANN *looks from the plate to William. There is a pregnant pause*)

I'll get a brush and sweep that up.

(WILLIAM *tosses the name-plate on to the sofa, crosses and exits* R. ANN *glowers after him, then crosses to the fireplace and wrenches the lead from the socket*)

ANN (*shouting*) For heaven's sake, don't bother. You've done enough damage already. Just take your wretched cleaner and go. (*She coils the cable and drops it on to the cleaner*) You blunder into the wrong house, probably the worse for drink, you deliberately ruin my new hearthrug—I ought to call the police.

(WILLIAM *enters* R, *looking very serious. He carries a dustpan and brush*)

WILLIAM. You're right—you ought.

ANN. What?

WILLIAM. Call in the police. I'm worried. (*He moves to the fireplace and brushes the hearthrug*)

ANN. You're worried! (*She crosses to William and hurriedly grabs the dustpan and brush*) Give me that, you'll only rub it in. (*She glares at him, and sweeps up the mess*)

WILLIAM (*picking up the name-plate and looking thoughtfully at it*) Just suppose this really is "Appleby".

ANN (*loudly*) Will you please go?

WILLIAM (*moving above the sofa*) This is the point—who was the fellow who let me in? (*He puts the name-plate on the table*)

ANN. How do I know? (*She suddenly rises, leaving the dustpan and brush on the hearthrug*) Did someone let you in? Someone must have!

WILLIAM (*picking up Montague's bowler*) Here's his bowler. He left it behind.

ANN. You're sure it isn't yours?

(WILLIAM *puts the hat on his head. It is much too small for him*)

WILLIAM. Well, there you are. (*He removes the hat and looks inside it*) Exhibit A—one gentleman's bowler hat, size six and five-eighths. Owner evidently suffers from dandruff. (*He sniffs*) Must be either Denis Compton or Robert Beatty. (*He replaces the hat on the back of the sofa*)

ANN. That's a tremendous help.

WILLIAM. It's almost all we have to go on. This—and the blood on the carpet.

ANN (*startled*) What?

WILLIAM (*pointing to the floor* LC) There.

ANN. Oh! (*She crosses to* LC *and peers cautiously at the stain on the carpet*) Where did it come from?

WILLIAM. I don't know. There's some more on the leg of the piano.

ANN. Are you certain it's blood?

WILLIAM. I'm afraid so.

ANN. But it can't be—not in St John's Wood.

WILLIAM. Murders have to happen somewhere.

ANN. *Murder?*

WILLIAM. Of course, that's taking an extreme view.

ANN (*looking fearfully about her*) You haven't found—anything have you?

WILLIAM. Not yet.

ANN. Why didn't you tell me before?

WILLIAM. We had to settle where the hell we were first.

ANN. I'm sure there must be some perfectly simple explanation—there always is.

WILLIAM. Maybe. Though on the other hand—well, never mind, let it go. (*He puts on his hat, kneels by his case and packs the cleaner into it*) After all, it's only a theory—so far.

ANN (*stopping him*) You're not going? I mean, if anything has happened I ought to know more about it.

WILLIAM (*rising*) Yes. I see your point. (*He removes his hat and puts it on the table up* RC)
ANN. Do you really think anything has?
WILLIAM. I'm bound to say it looks like it.
ANN. Oh—please don't go. Won't you sit down?
WILLIAM (*crossing and sitting on the sofa*) Thank you very much. (*He takes a packet of cigarettes and matches from his pocket*) Do you mind if I smoke?
ANN. Of course not. (*She pauses*) Well?
WILLIAM (*lighting a cigarette for himself*) I don't want to reopen a painful subject——

(ANN *hurriedly picks up the ashtray from the table* LC, *moves to the sofa and pointedly puts the ashtray on the sofa arm beside William*)

—but I'm perfectly certain that the name over that door read "Windyridge" when I first got here. I remember a scratch on the paint.
ANN. But you've just seen. It's "Appleby".
WILLIAM. "Appleby"—*now*. Suppose someone changed them over?
ANN. Why?
WILLIAM. Let's call the victim X.
ANN. The victim?
WILLIAM. The body. The corpse. X has arranged to call on someone at "Windyridge". Somebody else—probably the man who let me in—(*he indicates the bowler hat*) is very anxious indeed that X should never get there. (*He rises, moves above the sofa to the table and picks up the name-plate*) So he takes this and sticks it over the porch of "Windyridge" and brings this back here. He then lies in wait in this room until X comes along, looking for the real "Windyridge". She sees the name over the door . . .
ANN. She?
WILLIAM (*indicating the umbrella*) Exhibit B. The victim's umbrella, lady's model. Well, Miss X sees the name over the door, rings the bell, and he—Dandruff—lets her in. And that, madam, is how you came by your bloody carpet.
ANN (*shivering*) It sounds terribly convincing.
WILLIAM. Thank you. One of my previous occupations was writing detective stories.
ANN. But what did he do with—with her afterwards?
WILLIAM. We don't know yet. But our friend, having disposed of Miss X, is about to make his getaway when an unknown factor turns up.
ANN. What's that?
WILLIAM. Me. He doesn't know that I have made an appointment with Mrs Bostock. So without knowing it I find myself face to face with a murderer. His position is worse—he finds himself face to face with me. I try to sell him a vacuum cleaner—naturally

he doesn't feel like one at the moment. His nerve breaks, he make his escape by the back door, taking the precaution of changing back the name-plates on the way.

ANN. What happened then?

WILLIAM. I'm afraid the picture has reached the point where you came in. It fits, doesn't it?

ANN. Yes. But surely . . .

WILLIAM. What I can't understand is why he should choose this particular house to do it in.

ANN. I'm afraid that fits, too. You see, we haven't occupied it yet.

WILLIAM. We?

ANN. Myself and my fiancé.

WILLIAM. Oh!

ANN. We shan't be living here until after our wedding.

WILLIAM. How refreshing.

ANN (*coldly*) I meant that if whoever it was knew the house was unoccupied, he'd think he'd be perfectly safe.

WILLIAM. You've hit it. He was relying on the fact that he could leave her here undiscovered for days.

ANN. In that case, she—Miss X, that is . . . ?

WILLIAM (*apprehensively*) Cannot be far away.

ANN. Oughtn't we to call the police?

WILLIAM. Not without the evidence. Ridiculous though it may seem there's just the possibility that I may be wrong. I have a romantic streak in my nature that sometimes leads me astray.

ANN. I suppose I have, too, in a way.

WILLIAM. Really?

ANN (*hopefully*) You don't think we've both been led astray?

WILLIAM. Not in any worthwhile sense. (*He avoids her eye, moves away and ferrets about*)

ANN. What are you going to do?

WILLIAM. Search this room, with your permission. You take your side, I'll take this. Yell if you find anything.

ANN. Don't worry—I will. (*She brightens as a thought strikes her*) She might have got out.

WILLIAM. Out of what?

ANN. The house. Got away.

WILLIAM. It's possible. But in that case, one would expect to find a trail of blood to the window or the door. Depending, of course, on the nature and situation of the wound.

ANN. Don't!

WILLIAM. I'm sorry. At one time I used to be a medical student. I remember once in the dissecting room . . .

ANN. What? I thought you wrote stories.

WILLIAM. That was a spare-time occupation. (*He pauses*) We seem to have drawn a blank in here. (*He moves suddenly to the door* R)

ANN. Where are you going?

WILLIAM. A happy thought has just struck me.
ANN. What?
WILLIAM. She might be in the fridge.

(WILLIAM *exits* R. ANN *shudders and looks unhappily about. She crosses hurriedly to the mantelpiece, takes a cigarette from the packet on it and is nervously lighting the cigarette when she suddenly starts and looks towards the front door.*
WILLIAM *re-enters* R)

She's not in the fridge. What's the matter?
ANN (*gasping*) The door. Somebody's trying to get in. Supposing he's armed?

(WILLIAM *turns to look at the front door and there is the sound of a key turning in the lock*)

WILLIAM. Quick—behind the settee.

(WILLIAM *pulls* ANN *on to the floor behind the sofa.*
REGINALD *enters by the front door. He is dressed with extreme care, wearing a bowler and carrying a neatly furled umbrella. Under his arm he has two brown paper parcels, a picture wrapped in green baize and a large envelope. He throws the envelope on the sofa, crosses to the piano and lays the picture, hat and umbrella on it.* WILLIAM *and* ANN *creep on all fours to the stairs.* REGINALD *places the two parcels on the window seat, then turns and sees William and Ann*)

REGINALD. Ann!
ANN (*relieved*) Reginald!
REGINALD. Ann—what does this mean?

(WILLIAM *and* ANN, *suddenly becoming aware of the absurdity of their position, scramble to their feet.* REGINALD *stares, open-mouthed*)

ANN. Oh, Reginald, you're just in time.
REGINALD (*crossing to* C) So it appears. Who is this fellow?
ANN (*crossing to* R *of Reginald*) It's Mr —— (*She turns to William*) What was the name?
WILLIAM (*moving below the sofa*) Blake—William Blake. No relation to the famous admiral of course. You remember the old song about Blake tying a broom to the mast to sweep the Dutch off the sea.
ANN. Except that it was Van Tromp.
WILLIAM. Van Tromp what?
ANN. Van Tromp fixed the broom to his mast. Blake fixed a whip.
WILLIAM. No, I'm sure you're wrong about that. There's an old song about it. (*He sings*) "Now Blake was an admiral brave and bold . . ."
REGINALD (*breaking in*) Ann! What is all this?
ANN (*to William*) This is my fiancé. Reginald Willoughby-Pratt.

WILLIAM. I beg your pardon?
ANN (*clearly*) Reginald Willoughby-Pratt.
WILLIAM. I see.
REGINALD. Ann, I am still waiting for your explanation.
WILLIAM. May *I* explain? I came here to demonstrate a vacuum cleaner and . . .
REGINALD. That's hardly what you were doing when I came in.
ANN. You see, I'd forgotten you were coming over.
REGINALD. Apparently.
ANN. We were only hiding, Reginald.
REGINALD (*staring*) Hiding? From me?
ANN. No—him.
REGINALD. Who?
ANN. Mr Bostock.
WILLIAM. Not that he's really Mr Bostock, of course.
ANN. Because it's the wrong house.
WILLIAM. That's right.

(REGINALD *looks from one to the other as if he doubts not only their sanity, but his own*)

ANN. But whoever it was, we think he did it.
WILLIAM. At least, the evidence seems to point to it.
ANN. So you see, that's why.
REGINALD. Have you gone out of your mind?
ANN. But I've just told you—there's been a murder.
REGINALD. Murder? Where?
ANN. Here, we think—that is, he thinks.
REGINALD. You mean, in my house?
WILLIAM. Yes.
REGINALD. Rot!
ANN. How can you say that when you haven't heard his story?
REGINALD (*pompously*) Ann!
ANN (*subsiding*) I'm sorry, Reginald.
REGINALD (*to William*) Now could we have one thing at a time? And do please try to be coherent.
WILLIAM. Well, it was like this. I made an appointment with Mrs Bostock of "Windyridge". I saw the name over this door, and . . .
REGINALD. But this is not "Windyridge".
WILLIAM. If you don't mind, we've exhausted that topic. The door was open, I came in——
ANN. —and found *blood* on the carpet.
REGINALD (*looking quickly at the carpet*) Blood! Where?
WILLIAM (*pointing to the floor* LC) There. And there's some more on the leg of the piano.
ANN. And that's not all, Reginald. He found a man here.
WILLIAM. Pretending to be Mr Bostock.

B

REGINALD. Bostock?

ANN (*excitedly*) He wasn't actually Mr Bostock, of course, because the real Mr Bostock would be Mrs Bostock's husband, if she has one alive, which naturally we don't know as we've never met her, but she might have, in which case there would be two of them, but only one real one.

REGINALD (*who seems to be stunned by this*) I don't feel I can bring myself to ask you to say that again, Ann.

ANN. But, Reginald, it's frightfully important.

REGINALD. Of course, my dear. Now don't you think you ought to sit down for a while and relax? (*To William*) Please go on.

WILLIAM. The man disappeared while I was fixing the machine. I've no idea who he was.

REGINALD (*crossing to the fireplace*) That at least is clear. (*He suddenly spots the mess on the hearth rug*) Good heavens! What's that?

WILLIAM. An oversight. I was giving a demonstration and didn't know there was no juice. But you're right. Don't let's confuse the issue. I called Dandruff but . . .

REGINALD. You called who?

WILLIAM. Dandruff.

REGINALD. Dandruff?

WILLIAM (*picking up Montague's bowler and handing it to Reginald*) A *nom-de-chapeau* for Mr Bostock. I searched the house but he had gone all right. Then Miss . . . (*To Ann*) I don't think I ever had the pleasure?

ANN. Vincent—Ann Vincent.

WILLIAM. Ann Vincent. Hm! Pity to change it.

(REGINALD *glares at William*)

REGINALD. What?

WILLIAM (*catching Reginald's eye; quickly*) As I was saying, Miss Vincent arrived and found me looking for the body.

REGINALD. What body?

WILLIAM (*picking up the umbrella*) To go with this. Miss Vincent was quick to point out that I had come to the wrong house. (*He replaces the umbrella*) This wasn't "Windyridge", it was . . .

REGINALD }
ANN } (*together*) "Appleby".

REGINALD. Ann, please.

(ANN *sits in the easy chair* LC)

WILLIAM (*laughing*) "Appleby"—what a ridiculous name for a house.

REGINALD (*sharply*) Appleby happens to have been my mother's maiden name.

WILLIAM. I see the connection. I went to look over the porch, and sure enough it said "Appleby".
REGINALD. And what did you expect it to say?
WILLIAM. "Windyridge", of course—like it did when I got here. The name-plates had been deliberately changed over.
REGINALD (*raising his eyebrows*) Really? With what object may I ask?
WILLIAM. To decoy the lady with the umbrella here in the belief that this was "Windyridge". Hence the blood. This house was chosen because it hasn't been occupied yet. By the way, may I offer my congratulations?
REGINALD. Thank you. (*He studies the bowler hat and pulls out pieces of a newspaper which have been used to line it*)
ANN. Reginald, you really must do something. I'm sure we ought to call in the police.
REGINALD. Now, now, Ann. (*To William*) Is that all?
WILLIAM. Isn't it enough?
REGINALD. I should say it's altogether too much.
ANN. Aren't you going to do anything?
REGINALD. Nothing at all.
ANN. But, Reginald . . .
REGINALD. I never heard such tarradiddle in my life. I refuse to believe that anything in your story has the slightest criminal significance whatsoever.
WILLIAM. What? My dear sir . . .
REGINALD. These things simply don't happen.
WILLIAM. Oh! Don't you ever read the newspapers?
REGINALD. In my position that is hardly necessary.
ANN (*with pride*) Reginald is an announcer at the B.B.C.
WILLIAM. Television or disembodied?
REGINALD. If I may say so, you have built up an absurdly melodramatic picture which the events cannot for one moment justify.
WILLIAM. Can you explain them any better?
REGINALD. I think I can. Let us go back to the moment when you first thought you saw the name "Windyridge" over this porch. Where were you then?
WILLIAM. On the other side of the road.
REGINALD. Did you cross immediately?
WILLIAM. Let me think—yes, almost—I only waited for a lorry to pass. To be exact, it was a brewer's lorry. I remember feeling thirsty at the time.
REGINALD. You're sure of that?
WILLIAM. I think so.
REGINALD. Or did you, as one often does—note this carefully, Ann—did you walk a little way back along the pavement to cross *behind* the lorry?
WILLIAM. I might have done. Come to think of it, I did.

REGINALD. As I thought.
ANN. What do you mean, Reginald?
REGINALD. It's really very simple, my dear. Blake went back to pass behind the lorry, so that when he reached *our* side of the road he was then opposite *this* gate instead of the one next door.
WILLIAM. Where does that get us?
REGINALD. Perhaps I should have told you that the house next door is "Windyridge".
WILLIAM. Good Lord!
ANN. Is it?
REGINALD. Of course, my dear. (*To William*) Not realizing your mistake, you came up the garden path and into this house.
ANN (*gazing admiringly at Reginald*) Reginald, that's simply wonderful.
REGINALD. Just practical commonsense, my dear.
WILLIAM. Yes, but what about Mr Bostock?
ANN (*rising*) Yes—because of course we still don't know who Mr Bostock is except that he probably isn't . . .
REGINALD (*hurriedly interrupting*) For goodness' sake, Ann—the very mention of the name seems to make you gibber. (*To William*) Describe him.
WILLIAM. Let's see. Nondescript, thin-faced, thirty-ish, medium height . . .
REGINALD. Yes, yes, quite. One moment, please. (*He moves to the table up* RC, *sniffs at the glass and turns round the bottle, setting his thumb against the level of the liquid*) You haven't by any chance been helping yourself to my whisky?
WILLIAM. Certainly not.
ANN (*quite indignantly*) Of course he hasn't.
REGINALD (*crossing to* C) Well, someone has.
WILLIAM. Mr Bostock?
REGINALD. Precisely. Furthermore—(*he holds up the bits of paper he pulled out of the bowler hat*) he lines his hat with the racing edition of the *Star*. Putting two and two together, your friend Bostock is addicted to other people's whisky and the turf. Agreed?
WILLIAM. Well—oh, all right—so far.
REGINALD (*to Ann; brightly*) Now, my dear. Think. A nondescript man, thin-faced, thirty-ish, of medium height, who drinks whisky and backs horses. Who does this suggest to you? I'm sure we both have the same man in mind.

(ANN *thinks, then she gets it*)

ANN. Hackett!
REGINALD. Precisely. Hackett.
WILLIAM. Who's Hackett?
ANN. Mrs Hackett's husband. Mrs Hackett is our charwoman.
REGINALD (*putting the hat and pieces of newspaper on the table* RC) And probably the owner of that umbrella. A few days ago I

gave Hackett some odd jobs to do. Obviously he came here this afternoon to do them.

WILLIAM. Then what about the blood on the carpet?

REGINALD. One of the odd jobs was unpacking some glassware. Probably he broke something, cut himself, bled on our new carpet, then drank some of my whisky to steady his nerves.

ANN. Or else drank the whisky first and then broke something.

(*They all laugh*)

REGINALD. As I see it, your arrival no doubt caught him in the act, and he cleared out as soon as your back was turned. Well, I think that covers everything.

ANN. Reginald, you're marvellous, you really are.

WILLIAM. I must hand it to you. A very sound piece of reasoning.

REGINALD. I must say, Mr Blake, I think you should have thought twice before alarming Miss Vincent by inventing such a ridiculous story.

ANN. He didn't exactly invent it, dear. I mean, after all, it was quite a natural mistake to make. We can't all explain things away as cleverly as you do.

WILLIAM. There are heights to which some of us can never aspire.

REGINALD. Perhaps I was unjust. But in future, Blake, remember to look for the obvious explanation first. (*To Ann*) Well, my dear, if Mr Blake is satisfied, I don't think we need detain him any longer. (*He crosses to the table* RC *and pours a drink for himself*)

WILLIAM. Very well. (*He crosses to* C. *To Ann*) I'm sorry if I alarmed you over nothing.

ANN. That's all right. In a way it was quite fun. (*She hesitates, then turns to Reginald*) Perhaps Mr Blake would like a drink before he leaves.

WILLIAM. No, thank you. I'd be quite content if you would grant me one small favour.

REGINALD. What's that?

WILLIAM (*picking up the tube of the vacuum with a small attachment*) Your undivided attention for one moment. I have here the Electro-Broom, the Little Wizard of the Carpet.

REGINALD. I'm sorry, but I'm afraid we're not interested. (*He drains his glass, then crosses to* R *of Ann*)

WILLIAM. Ah, but no newly-married couple can afford to be without it. Picture it—the Electro-Broom's gentle, soothing hum will, in the years to come, drift upwards to the nursery like a lullaby and bring soft soothing slumber to the little tousled heads on the pillows.

REGINALD. Mr Blake, I have already given you your *congé*.

WILLIAM (*looking around*) I must have put it down somewhere.

ANN. Reginald, I do think it's the least we can do just to listen a moment to what he has to say.

WILLIAM. Thank you.
ANN. Even if it's utterly pointless.
WILLIAM. I—well now, the ordinary cleaner sweeps as it cleans . . . (*During the ensuing dialogue, he vainly endeavours to demonstrate the Electro-Broom*)
REGINALD (*glancing at his watch*) Good heavens! Look at the time. I've got to get back to Broadcasting House. I don't know what I'm going to do.
WILLIAM. You could put on a gramophone record.
REGINALD (*to Ann*) I haven't hung a single one of my pictures yet.
ANN. I'll do it for you afterwards.
REGINALD. But I know exactly how I want them.
WILLIAM. The superior cleaner beats as it . . .
ANN. You tell me how and I'll put them up.
REGINALD. But I've brought my "Mill House and Pool" with me—you know, the "attributed to Constable".
ANN. Well, there can't be more than one or two different ways of hanging pictures.
REGINALD (*crossing to the piano*) That just shows your complete unawareness of these things. (*He unwraps the painting*)
WILLIAM (*crossing to Reginald*) Perhaps I could be of assistance?
REGINALD. I hardly think so.
WILLIAM (*holding the vacuum tube to Reginald like a microphone*) Would you care to say a few words?
ANN. But Reginald, you just said that you had to get back to the B.B.C. and you want the pictures hung.
REGINALD. You don't think I'd trust *him* with my "attributed to Constable"?
WILLIAM (*looking at the picture; unimpressed*) Who attributed it?
ANN (*crossing down L*) We could leave that one out.
WILLIAM. We certainly could. Now, if you want to get under sofas . . .
REGINALD. I tell you, they will have to wait.
ANN. But Mr Blake has very kindly offered . . .
REGINALD. And I have refused. Besides, he'd knock holes in the walls.
WILLIAM. Do you know any other way of getting a nail in?
ANN. You'll be late, anyway.
REGINALD (*suspiciously*) You seem very anxious to get rid of me. (*He puts the picture on the piano*)
ANN. You just said you had to be going.
REGINALD. Is that the only reason?
ANN. What are you suggesting?
REGINALD. I don't think I need particularize.
ANN. Take that back at once!
REGINALD. Certainly—when you have got rid of this fellow.
ANN. I'll do nothing of the kind.

REGINALD. Very well! (*He picks up his hat and puts it on*) I shall go back to Broadcasting House. (*He picks up his umbrella, crosses to the front door, opens it, then turns and pauses dramatically*) I'm just beginning to realize the true significance of the little scene that greeted my entrance. Good-bye.

ANN (*crossing to Reginald*) How—how *dare* you! Good-bye.

(REGINALD *exits by the front door, slamming it behind him. The cupboard door springs open and the mop falls out*)

(*She screams, then replaces the mop and closes the cupboard door*) He had absolutely no right to say that.

WILLIAM. Certainly not. He should know you better.

ANN (*moving down* C) He should indeed.

WILLIAM (*moving to* L *of Ann*) Of course this is absolutely nothing to do with me—but may I make a suggestion? Always stand up to Reginald like that. It'll do him good.

ANN. I certainly will.

WILLIAM. Speaking out of turn—as someone on the outside looking in—he seems to think he's marrying an echo.

ANN. Well, he's not. He should never have said that—never. Even if he didn't really mean it.

WILLIAM. Now, don't weaken.

ANN. I'm not. He simply goaded me into answering him back, didn't he?

WILLIAM. Unquestionably.

ANN (*after a pause*) I'll bet he'll be feeling sorry when he cools down.

WILLIAM (*putting the vacuum tube in the case*) Only for himself.

ANN. How can you say that? You've only known him five minutes.

WILLIAM. He's been saying good night to me on the air for the last five years.

ANN (*unhappily*) He'll have reached the end of the road by now.

WILLIAM. Oozing self-pity.

(ANN *suddenly looks very hard at* WILLIAM *who looks at the ceiling*)

ANN. I believe you're deliberately trying to make things worse. Anyway, everything's gone wrong since you turned up.

WILLIAM. Did I choose Reginald for you?

ANN. That's nothing to do with it.

WILLIAM. As a complete outsider, I can't very well comment. Otherwise I might remark that it's everything to do with it.

ANN. What do you mean?

WILLIAM. You two haven't a hope. He's a realist—you're a romantic.

ANN. Now you're being impertinent!

WILLIAM. I was only trying to help in a spirit of scrupulous detachment.

ANN. You mean, you're trying to detach me from Reginald.
WILLIAM. I won't say any more. It will only be misunderstood.
ANN. I was a fool to have listened to your cock-and-bull story in the first place. (*She moves towards the front door*)
WILLIAM. Where are you going?
ANN. I'm going to catch my fiancé before he reaches the station. And when I come back I expect to find you gone—and my hearthrug cleaned up. You've messed up my house, but you're not going to ruin my life.

(ANN *flings out by the front door, slamming it after her.* WILLIAM *shrugs and turns his attention to packing his vacuum cleaner, but the tube proves difficult to get into the box, and he flings it down in disgust. He crosses to the fireplace to clean the hearthrug. As he picks up the dust pan, the soot Ann has already swept up falls on to the rug. He gives this up, too, in disgust and wanders* C. *Seeing the picture on the piano, he picks it up and singing to himself, "Blake was an Admiral . . ." tries the picture in various positions on the walls. Losing the tune of his song, he puts the picture on the floor by the window, turns to the piano, puts one knee on the piano stool and with one finger he plays the melody. As it rises to the B flat, the piano emits only a clicking sound*)

WILLIAM (*murmuring*) That's funny.

WILLIAM *plays the tune again, but on the same note, the same thing happens again. He takes his knee from the stool, lifts the lid of the piano and looks inside. A woman's arm* flops inertly over the downstage side of the piano. He lowers the lid and crosses to* C. *As he does so, he realizes with something approaching an electric shock what has happened. He trembles all over, emitting terrified whimpers, rushes half-way up the stairs, then down again and out of the front door. He runs in again almost immediately, crosses to the piano, lifts the lid, and without looking, pops the arm back inside, then bolts out of the front door as—*

the CURTAIN *falls*

---

* See note on page 77.

To face page 21—Meet A Body *Photograph by Houston Rogers*

ACT II

Scene 1

SCENE—*The lounge of the house next door. Immediately following.*

The room is similar to the lounge of "Appleby" except that there is no staircase, the space being filled with a set of built-in book-shelves; the fireplace is of different design, there are french windows instead of casement, and the room is fully furnished. There is a cabinet for drinks down L, a sofa LC, *an armchair by the fireplace and a table with upright chairs* R *and* L *of it stands* RC. *A console table stands in front of the bookshelves and the room is lit by a standard lamp up* RC, *a table lamp on the cabinet* L *and wall-brackets over the fireplace. There is a tape recorder on the console table up* RC, *and a hall stand* R *of the front door. A telephone stands on a small table* L *of the alcove up* C.

(*See the Ground Plan and Photograph of the scene*)

When the CURTAIN *rises,* MR HAWKINS *and* POLICE SERGEANT BASSET *are seated at the table* RC, *playing chess.* HAWKINS *is a shaggy man, aged fifty-five or so, cultured and a little old-womanish. His manner is mild and inoffensive. He is seated* R *of the table, the* SERGEANT L *of it. It is apparently* HAWKINS' *move.*

HAWKINS. I'm sorry to keep you waiting, Sergeant.
SERGEANT. That's all right, sir. Take your time.

(*An antique clock on the mantelpiece chimes seven*)

(*He glances at the clock*) Pretty chime that clock's got.
HAWKINS. Mmm.
SERGEANT. Make it yourself, sir?
HAWKINS. Scarcely. It dates from seventeen-sixty. I only reconstructed it.
SERGEANT. Rare lot of skill that needs I should think, all the same.
HAWKINS. It's my job.

(*For a moment they study the board in silence*)

I think, I think I can see something. That's the trouble with me, I'm always thinking I think I can see something.
SERGEANT. Well, Mr Hawkins, perhaps you can.
HAWKINS. What?
SERGEANT. See something.
HAWKINS (*roguishly*) A police trap—eh?
SERGEANT. Now you know I wouldn't deceive *you*, Mr Hawkins.

HAWKINS. Hm. Well, perhaps you haven't this time. (*Rather pleased with himself he makes a move*) There, we'll try that.
SERGEANT (*looking at Hawkins in some surprise*) Oh!
HAWKINS. Bit of a surprise, eh?
SERGEANT. Would you like that move back, sir?
HAWKINS. Eh! What's the matter?
SERGEANT. Mate in two more moves for me, I'm afraid.
HAWKINS. How do you make that out?
SERGEANT (*rapidly*) My bishop to here, check, you can't move here or here or here, so you'll have to move here. I move my queen here, check and you've had it. Q.E.D.
HAWKINS. Mate?
SERGEANT. Mate.
HAWKINS (*sighing*) And I thought I was being *such* a Machiavelli.
SERGEANT. Like it back?
HAWKINS. Oh no, no.
SERGEANT. Go on, have it back.
HAWKINS. No, no, it would be bad for my character. Besides . . . (*He makes a vague gesture towards the clock*)
SERGEANT (*rising*) Yes, I'm afraid you're right. (*He moves to the hall stand and collects his helmet and bicycle clips*)
HAWKINS (*rising*) One for the road?
SERGEANT (*putting on his helmet*) Not when I'm going on duty, if you don't mind, sir. Thanks for the game. You did a bit better this time.
HAWKINS. You're much too clever for me, I'm afraid, Sergeant. Same time next week, then. Meanwhile, don't let them promote you out of the district, Sergeant.
SERGEANT. Promotion? Fat chance of that! (*He puts the bicycle clips round his trouser legs*)
HAWKINS. Come, merit must tell sooner or later.
SERGEANT (*crossing to the door* R) Merit don't enter into it very far, Mr Hawkins. Only luck. Happening to be on the spot when something juicy breaks. But somehow or other I never am. Never. Good night, sir.

(*The* SERGEANT *exits* R. HAWKINS *crosses to the cabinet* L, *takes his pipe from his pocket and fills it from the tobacco jar on the cabinet*)

(*Off*) Good night, Nellie.
MRS BOSTOCK'S VOICE (*off*) Good night, Sergeant. Mind how you go on that bike of yours.

(*There is a violent knocking on the front door.* HAWKINS *crosses to the front door and opens it, revealing a very agitated* WILLIAM *on the threshold*)

WILLIAM (*without any preliminaries; excitedly*) Where's your telephone?

HAWKINS. Eh?
WILLIAM (*pushing past Hawkins into the room*) Telephone?
HAWKINS (*moving to L of William*) May I ask . . . ?
WILLIAM. Couldn't find a call box. Where is it?
HAWKINS. What *is* all this?
WILLIAM. Next door. We must call the police.
HAWKINS. The police?
WILLIAM. Murder.
HAWKINS. What?
WILLIAM. Next door. Just found a body.
HAWKINS. Good gracious!
WILLIAM. A woman.
HAWKINS. No!
WILLIAM. Where's the phone?
HAWKINS. Oh dear! You've just missed the police sergeant. He was here only a minute ago. Playing chess, mated me in two. Telephone, yes, yes, the telephone. (*He turns to the table up LC and lifts the telephone receiver*)
WILLIAM. Hurry.
HAWKINS. Yes, of course. Which side?
WILLIAM. That side, "Appleby".
HAWKINS. "Appleby". A woman?
WILLIAM. Yes. Dial nine-nine-nine.
HAWKINS (*struggling with the dial*) Nine-nine . . . Wait a minute, better if I catch Sergeant Basset at the station. Now what's the number? Oh, yes. (*To William*) Oh—would you mind closing the front door. (*He dials*)

(WILLIAM, *in his agitation, closes the front door from outside, thereby locking himself out. He knocks violently and* HAWKINS *re-admits him*)

You're quite serious about this?
WILLIAM. Of course. (*He shuts the front door*)
HAWKINS. Yes. I must say you look it. (*Into the telephone*) Oh, police station . . . Yes . . . Oh—good evening. Is Sergeant Basset there yet? . . . Mr Hawkins . . . I know he's on his way. He can't be more than a moment . . . Yes, I'll hang on. (*To William*) Couldn't be suicide?
WILLIAM. Out of the question.
HAWKINS. Mm. (*Into the telephone*) Sergeant? . . . Oh, thank goodness. You must come back here at once. There's been a death next door and the young man thinks it's murder . . . What? The man who found the body . . . Yes, next door.
WILLIAM. "Appleby".
HAWKINS. "Appleby" . . . Oh, yes, do, please . . . Yes, of course. (*He listens for a moment, then replaces the receiver*) He's coming round at once.
WILLIAM. How long will he be?
HAWKINS. Two or three minutes at the most.

WILLIAM. Good.
HAWKINS. Meanwhile he says everything is to be left exactly as you found it. (*He crosses to the cabinet* L) Do sit down and let me get you something.
WILLIAM. Thank you. I won't say no.
HAWKINS. Rather not. Try to relax. (*He pours a drink for William*) I didn't know the people next door had moved in yet.
WILLIAM (*crossing to Hawkins*) They're on the verge—just finishing furnishing.
HAWKINS (*turning with the bottle and glass in his hands*) I see.

(WILLIAM *turns to take the drink, but grabs the bottle instead*)

WILLIAM. Thanks. (*He exchanges the bottle for the glass*) Oh—sorry.
HAWKINS (*replacing the bottle on the cabinet*) And you—pardon me, but I suppose in the circumstances I ought to ask . . .
WILLIAM (*sitting on the sofa*) I'm just a salesman who happened to have an appointment. Stumbled on the thing by accident.
HAWKINS (*crossing to* C) It must have been a nasty shock.
WILLIAM. It was.
HAWKINS. Most upsetting. It upsets me just to hear about it. And the victim, was—it—I should say—she . . . ?
WILLIAM. I don't know. Never seen her before in my life.
HAWKINS. Dear me. Hmm! In the circumstances I had better tell my housekeeper she can go for the night. These local people talk so. What do you think?
WILLIAM. I expect you're right.
HAWKINS. She won't think anything being a daily woman. (*He crosses to the door* R *and calls*) We shan't want anything more tonight, you can go if you want to.
MRS BOSTOCK'S VOICE (*off*) Thank you, Mr Hawkins. The usual time in the morning?
HAWKINS. Er—yes.
MRS BOSTOCK'S VOICE (*off in the distance*) Good night, sir.
HAWKINS (*calling*) Good night, Mrs Bostock.
WILLIAM (*looking up sharply*) Mrs *Bostock*?
HAWKINS. Yes.
WILLIAM. Then this is "Windyridge"?
HAWKINS. That's so. (*He picks up the box of cigarettes and matches from the table up* RC, *crosses and offers a cigarette to William*) Cigarette?
WILLIAM (*taking a cigarette*) Thank you. Good Lord! Of course it would be. (*Suddenly*) Were you expecting anybody tonight?
HAWKINS (*lighting William's cigarette*) I beg your pardon?
WILLIAM. A lady by any chance?
HAWKINS. I don't follow, why? (*He crosses and replaces the box and matches on the table* RC)
WILLIAM. I don't know whether . . . Well, there's no reason why I shouldn't tell you. I've reason to believe that the woman who

was killed was coming here.

HAWKINS. Oh, good gracious! What makes you think that?

WILLIAM. You'll hear the full story when the police come. I believe the name-plates on the porches were changed over for half an hour or so this evening. Yours was stuck over the porch next door. The victim called there thinking it was the real "Windyridge". Incidentally, so did I. I'd made a date with your Mrs Bostock to demonstrate a vacuum cleaner.

HAWKINS. *What?* But what a fantastic suggestion—not the vacuum cleaner itself, of course, that strikes a mundane note which seems *quite* out of keeping. But, my dear fellow, surely . . .

WILLIAM. You're certain nobody was calling here tonight?

HAWKINS. Only the police sergeant.

WILLIAM. Then I give it up.

HAWKINS. Unless . . . No, it couldn't be that.

WILLIAM. What?

HAWKINS. I've an unmarried sister living at Purley, who's apt to call without warning. But I really don't see . . .

WILLIAM. Did she paint her finger nails?

HAWKINS. Good gracious, no. Maud disapproves most strongly of . . .

WILLAIM (*interrupting*) Well, this one did.

HAWKINS. Oh, thank goodness for that. I must say for the moment you gave me quite a turn. You know I find it difficult to believe that one minute I'm playing chess with a policeman, the next I'm mixed up in murder most foul. I suppose I shall have to appear in court?

WILLIAM. To say nothing of the *News of the World*.

HAWKINS. Really? You think so? And I detest sensationalism in any form.

WILLIAM. It shook me, I don't mind telling you. Imagine opening a piano and seeing that.

HAWKINS. A piano?

WILLIAM. That's right.

HAWKINS. It—she was in a *pianoforte*?

WILLIAM. Yes.

HAWKINS. Good God! This is positively surrealist!

WILLIAM. Well, there she was as large as life and . . . (*He breaks off and rises*) Lord, I'd forgotten!

HAWKINS. What?

WILLIAM. Miss Vincent—the girl who lives next door—she doesn't know and she's coming back.

HAWKINS. You mean somebody ought to warn her?

WILLIAM. If she sees what I saw . . .

HAWKINS (*hurriedly*) Yes, quite—don't dwell on it. (*He coughs and eyes William*) One of us ought to go, I suppose?

WILLIAM. It had better be me.

HAWKINS. Oh, really—I wasn't trying to . . .

WILLIAM. Oh, that's all right.
HAWKINS. I admire your spirit I must say. I'll wait here for Sergeant Basset.

(WILLIAM *drains his glass in a final gulp*)

WILLIAM. Well, back to the Chamber of Horrors. (*He puts his glass on the cabinet* L *and crosses to the front door*)
HAWKINS (*stopping him*) Just a moment. Oughtn't you to take some weapon with you, just in case?
WILLIAM. What? Please don't put ideas into my head.
HAWKINS (*bumbling about*) We've nothing in the house to meet these situations, except the tools of my trade—I'm a clockmaker, you know. Ah—wait a minute. (*He moves to the console table up* RC, *opens the drawer and takes out a revolver of about eighteen-sixty vintage*) What about this?
WILLIAM (*recoiling*) Good Heavens!
HAWKINS. It *is* rather old. My great uncle acquired it when he lived in western America. He always used to say it gave him confidence—er—he was a rent collector.
WILLIAM (*gingerly taking the revolver from Hawkins*) Is it loaded?
HAWKINS. Oh, no, no. I don't think my great uncle ever actually fired the thing. I imagine he was thinking of the—er—visual effect.
WILLIAM (*returning the revolver to Hawkins*) Thanks. I think on the whole I'll be safer without it. I don't want the police to mistake me for the murderer. (*He moves to the front door*)
HAWKINS (*moving to the front door and opening it*) Good luck.
WILLIAM. Thanks. And before the sergeant comes back, please put away that chess board. I shall feel strongly about any delay.

(WILLIAM *exits by the front door.* HAWKINS *closes the front door and replaces the revolver in the drawer. As he does so, a low whistle is heard off* R. *It is repeated.*
HAWKINS *exits hurriedly* R)

HAWKINS (*off*) What the devil are you doing?

(*There is a muffled reply*)

(*Off*) Wait there. Wait!

(HAWKINS *re-enters, crosses to the window and draws the curtains so that the room is in near darkness.*
MONTAGUE *enters* R. *He carries a bundle wrapped in a dust sheet, over his shoulder, which can dimly be identified as the body of a woman*)

(*He points to the sofa. Sternly*) Over there.

(MONTAGUE *crosses and dumps the bundle on to the sofa.* HAWKINS *crosses to the light switch* R *of the alcove up* C *and switches on the lights*)

(*He gives a cursory glance at the body and turns on Montague*) I thought I told you to make certain the house next door was empty.

MONTAGUE. I did, but . . .

HAWKINS (*moving down* C) Then what the hell's happened? You've made an unholy mess of everything.

MONTAGUE. *I've* made an unholy mess! How was I to know that chap had made a date with Mrs Bostock?

HAWKINS. You could have got rid of him.

MONTAGUE. I'd like to have known what you'd have done.

HAWKINS. Bought his blasted vacuum cleaner, of course.

MONTAGUE. Where is he now?

HAWKINS. Next door, waiting for the police.

MONTAGUE (*alarmed*) Police? What the . . . ?

HAWKINS. It's all right. As it so happens they won't be coming. Reconnect the telephone, will you, there's a good fellow.

(MONTAGUE *moves to the telephone receiver, picks up the end of the lead and plugs it into the skirting board*)

MONTAGUE. Who disconnected it?

HAWKINS. I did, of course.

MONTAGUE (*moving to* L *of Hawkins*) Suppose Munro's been trying to get through?

HAWKINS. I could hardly discuss the removal of Sir Gregory Upshott in front of Police Sergeant Basset—it might have put him off his game. Surely even you can see that.

MONTAGUE (*suddenly bursting out*) I can't see what I'm not told —and I'm not told anything.

HAWKINS. What's this? Temperament? Temperament?

MONTAGUE. If you took me into your confidence instead of always keeping me in the dark . . .

HAWKINS. What's that to do with it, may I ask?

MONTAGUE. We're working for the same cause, aren't we?

HAWKINS. I always keep one shining ideal before me. Number One.

MONTAGUE. Look here, Mr Hawkins—I came into this because of my political convictions.

HAWKINS. Your convictions unfortunately have not been confined to the political.

MONTAGUE. All right, throw that in my face. You know I only agreed to come in on this because that bloke Upshott represents everything I hate—oil monopolists who grind the faces of the poor . . .

HAWKINS (*interrupting*) The trouble with you, Montague, is that you've developed your peculiar ideology at the expense of your brains. What is troubling you, my boy?

MONTAGUE. I've got a right to be properly informed.

HAWKINS. This passion of the working man for a share in management! Sometimes I wonder what we're coming to.

MONTAGUE. I did what you told me with her, didn't I?
HAWKINS (*glancing at the body*) Apparently.
MONTAGUE. I didn't ask any questions, then, did I?
HAWKINS. No. You were delightfully silent.
MONTAGUE. Although you didn't even tell me who she was.
HAWKINS. Didn't I?
MONTAGUE. You know you didn't.
HAWKINS (*glancing at the body; with a sigh*) Poor Winifred.
MONTAGUE. Winifred?
HAWKINS. Sir Gregory's secretary. She was good enough to give me the fullest particulars of her employer's movements and habits. Yes, in a way we owe everything to her.
MONTAGUE. So *she* was your stool-pigeon?
HAWKINS. Such a pity she smelt a rat. Imagine my indignation, when I discovered she was actually following *me*—and had even found out my address. You know me, honest and open to a fault. I taxed her with it only this afternoon when she telephoned. But she would insist on coming here at once. At such short notice, too, no time to put off Sergeant Basset. Poor Sergeant Basset! *Such an incompetent chess player!*

(MONTAGUE *glances nervously around*)

What *is* the matter?
MONTAGUE. Supposing that vacuum cleaner bloke comes back?
HAWKINS. That's unlikely for the next ten minutes. But if he does, then I'm afraid you'll have to repeat your earlier performance.
MONTAGUE. I don't like it. Everything's gone wrong. Let's get out of here while the going's good.
HAWKINS. Nothing's gone wrong that can't be put right. Meanwhile, I would like to run over the arrangements at Newcliffe. Must get it right after all. Let's see—the bar parlour at the *Green Man* is the first door on the right—and the radio set that you sold the landlord you put at the foot of the stairs.
MONTAGUE. That's right, on an old radiogram. You can't miss it. All you have to do is turn it round, take off the back, set the time clock and connect the detonator.
HAWKINS (*smiling*) I think I ought to be able to manage that.
MONTAGUE. It's not much of a pub. Not the sort of place you'd expect Upshott to patronize.
HAWKINS. He has his reasons for wishing to be discreet.
MONTAGUE. Oh, it's like that, is it?
HAWKINS. Sir Gregory has responded to the call of the wild in the shape of the fourth typist from the left in his outer office. Tonight he's taking her down to the *Green Man*—incognito, of course, as he's a public figure.

MONTAGUE. A public gilded sepulchre!

HAWKINS. Now, now, Montague, you mustn't let your ideology get the better of you. Still it does make a nice pattern, doesn't it? To stab him so to speak through the chink in his armour. We are striking in our humble way a blow for morality. Doesn't that make you happy?

MONTAGUE. All I'm concerned with is carrying out our orders.

HAWKINS. There's no need to be so damned virtuous. *You're* being paid for it, too.

MONTAGUE. I tell you, I'm only concerned with making quite certain Upshott never gets to the Middle East.

HAWKINS. With a little luck he might be blown there.

MONTAGUE. How do you know he'll be anywhere near the radio set?

HAWKINS (*moving to the tape recorder*) How do I know?

MONTAGUE. What have you got there?

HAWKINS. The answer to your question. A tape recorder. Excuse me.

(HAWKINS *starts the tape recorder working and as* SIR GREGORY'S *voice starts to come over on the loud-speaker,* HAWKINS *stop-watches the start. The recording commences in the middle of a sentence and is continuous during the ensuing dialogue. The speech is given in full at the end of the play.* HAWKINS *is resuming the timing of it, presumably interrupted*)

MONTAGUE. What's that?

HAWKINS. Don't you recognize Sir Gregory?

MONTAGUE (*staring at the machine*) What?

HAWKINS. It's his speech at the luncheon today. I took this off the broadcast.

MONTAGUE. This isn't the time to go playing records.

HAWKINS. The point is, Montague, they're broadcasting a recording of his speech, *this* speech—at ten forty-five tonight, and Sir Gregory, like most politicians, is known to be very fond of the sound of his own voice.

MONTAGUE. You mean he'll listen to it.

HAWKINS. It's a psychological certainty.

(*The telephone rings*)

Munro! Answer it. (*He continues to time the recording with his stopwatch*)

(MONTAGUE *moves to the telephone and lifts the receiver*)

MONTAGUE (*into the telephone*) Yes, Montague here . . . Yes, he is . . . What? . . . Good. All right . . . I'll tell him . . . What? . . . Going smoothly? . . . I wouldn't exactly say that . . . O.K. (*He replaces the receiver and turns to Hawkins*) Sir Gregory's on his way to Newcliffe.

HAWKINS. Splendid. Just a moment.

(HAWKINS *listens intently to the recording which at this point reaches* ". . . *when I will disappear this time finally, from the public scene*")

(*He checks the stop-watch and stops the recorder*) ". . . disappear, this time finally, from the public scene." And so he will, bless his little heart, at that most appropriate moment. Let's see—(*he consults his stop-watch*) three and five is eight—at ten forty-eight precisely. Ingenious, I think, on the whole.

MONTAGUE. It would be simpler to shoot him.

HAWKINS. So you have remarked on a wearisome number of occasions. Simpler perhaps, but not safer. (*He moves to the hall-stand and takes his overcoat from it*) Besides, I'm fond of any sort of mechanism. Even the human mechanism. (*He dons his overcoat*) I'll see you at Heath Row at seven in the morning.

MONTAGUE (*indicating the body*) What about her?

HAWKINS. Yes, that's a point. There's an inspection pit in the garage—I should think that would be quite a nice place. I'm sure I can rely on you not to linger. (*He puts on his hat and picks up a small attaché-case from the hall-stand*)

MONTAGUE. You bet.

(HAWKINS *moves to the front door*)

(*He moves quickly to Hawkins*) Wait a minute. (*He suddenly thrusts out his hand, with emotional stolidity*) Good luck to our Mission.

HAWKINS. When I look at you, Montague, I'm glad my mind is a political vacuum. (*He pauses as he turns again to go*) Do you know I feel quite excited. I honestly believe I'd do this sort of work without even being paid for it. I suppose if the truth be known I have a kink. Good night.

HAWKINS *exits by the front door, closing it after him.* MONTAGUE *stands for a moment, surveying the body. The sound of Hawkins' car is heard driving off, then* MONTAGUE *switches off the lights, crosses to the door* R, *rolls up his sleeves, in preparation for his grisly task and exits* R. *After a moment there is a faint groan from the sofa. The body writhes under the dust sheet shroud, then slowly struggles to sit upright as—*

the CURTAIN *falls*

SCENE 2

SCENE—*The same as Act I. The same evening.*

When the CURTAIN *rises, the room is exactly as at the end of Act I. The front door is open and the stage is empty. After a moment,* ANN *enters* by the front door. *She is hatless and rather breathless as if she had hurried up the road after leaving Reginald. She looks around as if expecting William to be there. She sees the vacuum cleaner still lying on the floor, stares indignantly at it, then glances around the room and crosses swiftly to the door* R.

ANN (*calling*) Hey, you! Are you still here?

(*There is no reply*)

(*She calls up the stairs*) Are you there? Hello! Mr Blake. Hello! (*She decides William must have gone, moves to* C *and looks at the vacuum cleaner. Then her attention is drawn to the parcels she brought in earlier. They are lying on the window seat. Her face lights up, she crosses quickly to the parcels, delves inside and pulls out a housecoat and a scanty foundation garment. She looks at the garment, and then glances around her as if in search of something. She picks up a mirror from the top of the packing chest, runs across with it to the mantelpiece and stands it up*)

(ANN, *after holding the garment briefly against her and peering in the mirror, exits hurriedly* R.

WILLIAM *enters by the front door. He glances around, and thinking Ann has not returned, studies the room curiously for a second, moves to the sofa, picks up the umbrella, then carefully takes up the bowler hat. He examines the interior of the hat, sniffs and makes a face. He crosses to the window, holds the bowler hat up to the light at arm's length and looks thoughtfully at it, at the same time drumming his fingers of one hand on top of the piano. Suddenly he realizes he is touching the piano where he saw the body. He jumps away from it, puts the hat and umbrella on the table* LC, *then glances around as if a thought had just struck him, crosses and exits up the stairs.*

ANN *re-enters* R. *She is now clothed in her foundation garment and housecoat. She crosses quickly to the front door, closes it, and feeling that she is now quite safe she moves* C *and with an air of freedom, swiftly takes off her housecoat, tosses it into the easy chair* LC, *and reveals herself in the foundation garment. She then moves the sofa in line with the mirror on the mantelpiece and, jumping on the sofa, balances on the arm and surveys herself in the mirror.*

WILLIAM, *as* ANN *is performing her difficult balancing feat, enters quickly and quietly down the stairs. Seeing Ann, he turns and bolts out of sight again, then re-enters, looking deliberately nonchalant.* ANN *does not see him*)

WILLIAM. Keeping fit?

ANN (*turning; startled*) Oh! (*She loses her balance and falls on to the sofa, quickly pulling a cushion down to cover herself up. Shrilly*) Where did you come from?

WILLIAM. Upstairs.

ANN. Why?

WILLIAM. Well, it's usually up there.

ANN. You have no business here at all. How long have you been standing there?
WILLIAM. Only a second or two. Not more. I didn't count.
ANN. Get me my wrap please, over there.
WILLIAM (*crossing to the easy chair*) Certainly. (*He picks up the housecoat, moves towards Ann, then stops short and throws the housecoat to her*)
ANN. Kindly turn your back.
WILLIAM. Yes. Of course. (*He turns smartly so that his back is to her*) Let me know when the lights turn green.
ANN. When I do, you can take your vacuum cleaner and clear out. (*She rises and dons her housecoat*)
WILLIAM. That's out of the question just now.
ANN. Very well then, I shall send for the police.
WILLIAM. That's why it's out of the question.
ANN. What?
WILLIAM. I've sent for them already.

(ANN *stares at him*)

Called them from next door.
ANN. Turn round.

(WILLIAM *turns mechanically*)

What did you say?
WILLIAM. Police Sergeant Basset is on his way to investigate the murder.
ANN. What murder?
WILLIAM. The one Reginald called off.
ANN. What about it?
WILLIAM. It's on again.

(ANN *stares at him and suddenly seems to realize that she is quite alone. She looks apprehensively at William and glances nervously about her*)

ANN. Oh—is it?
WILLIAM. Please don't be alarmed, I'm quite sane and it's perfectly true.
ANN. But Reginald explained it away.
WILLIAM. Reginald would explain anything away.
ANN. He tore your silly story to shreds and you know it. (*She takes the mirror from the mantelpiece and crosses to the window seat*)
WILLIAM. I'm afraid I've put it together again. (*He catches sight of himself in the mirror*) I say—who's that good-looking fellow following you?
ANN (*putting the mirror on the window seat*) Reginald was absolutely right. Of course he was right. (*She crosses to the hearth*) In spite of your cheap sneers he generally is right, because he has sense and intelligence and . . .

WILLIAM. But he hasn't got a body.
ANN. How dare you! (*She picks up the dust pan and brush and sweeps the hearthrug*)
WILLIAM. I was referring to the corpse.
ANN. So you have a corpse now?
WILLIAM. Yes. I found it while you were running after Reginald. So we are now back in position one.
ANN. Indeed?
WILLIAM. You think I'm lying, don't you?
ANN. In my opinion you're a pathological case.

(ANN *exits* R, *taking the dust pan and brush with her*)

WILLIAM (*crossing to the door* R *and calling*) Miss Vincent, you must understand that this is a serious matter. The police are on the way and the man who committed this murder is still at large. Perhaps only a few yards from us at this moment.

(ANN *enters* R *and stands in the doorway*)

ANN. What was that?
WILLIAM. What?
ANN. That whistle.
WILLIAM. What whistle?
ANN (*listening intently*) There's someone in the garden.
WILLIAM. Are you sure?
ANN. Listen.

(*They both pause and listen*)

They must be whistling to someone they think is in this house.
WILLIAM. Stay here. (*He strides quickly to the front door, opens it and stands just outside*)

(ANN *dashes to the front door and slams it shut*)

ANN (*shouting through the letter-box*) If you want your vacuum cleaner you can call back in the morning. I'll tell Mrs Hackett to put it out on the doorstep.

(WILLIAM *pushes the letter-box open and shouts through it from outside*)

WILLIAM. Hey, let me in.
ANN. Certainly not.
WILLIAM. Miss Vincent!
ANN. Stop making that noise and go away.
WILLIAM. It's important—open the door.
ANN. I will not.
WILLIAM. Remember there's a body in there.
ANN. I know, but it's got a vacuum cleaner already.
WILLIAM. Is that your final word?
ANN. Of course.

WILLIAM. Very well, I'll go. (*He closes the letter-box, then immediately reopens it*) You'll find it in the piano.
ANN. What?
WILLIAM (*grimly*) It. Good-bye. (*He closes the letter-box*)

(ANN *looks at the piano, then uncertainly at the front door. She moves hesitantly to the piano, fearfully touches the lid, starts to open it, then suddenly pulls her hand away, unable to go through with it. She hurries to the front door and opens it*)

ANN (*calling*) Mr. Blake!

(WILLIAM *instantly pops into view and steps quickly over the threshold*)

WILLIAM. Did you call?
ANN. If you said that just so that you could sneak back into this house . . .
WILLIAM. I give you my word. Would you like me to prove it? (*He crosses to the piano*) I must warn you that it won't be pleasant. (*He puts his hand on the lid to open it*)
ANN (*suddenly stopping him*) No—don't.
WILLIAM. If you'd rather not look . . . (*He again starts to raise the lid*)
ANN. Wait. (*She looks fearfully at him*) It *was* a woman? Wasn't it—after all?
WILLIAM. Yes, it was. She was murdered.
ANN. How do you know she was murdered?
WILLIAM. Well, people don't usually kill themselves and pop themselves into pianos.
ANN (*closing the front door*) Who could it be? I don't understand how it could possibly have happened here. (*She moves down* C)
WILLIAM. The police may be able to answer both those questions, I can't. The front door was locked, of course?
ANN. Naturally.
WILLIAM. Then the chap I met must have come in by the window. (*He turns to the window and looks at it*) Yes, this one's open.
ANN. You mean he came in—and waited?
WILLIAM. Yes. He must have opened the door to her.
ANN. Then she would have seen him.
WILLIAM. She probably expected to.
ANN. But when he attacked her, surely she would have screamed. Somebody would be bound to hear.
WILLIAM. He might have taken her by surprise.
ANN. How?
WILLIAM. This wants working out. He must have been in a position to . . . Sit down a minute.
ANN. Why?
WILLIAM. I'll show you.

(ANN *sits on the sofa*)

(*He crosses to* C) I sit opposite to you—here. (*He sits* L *of Ann on the sofa*) Let's say you're trying to blackmail me.

ANN. Why?
WILLIAM. Well, I have a wife and children.
ANN. Have you?
WILLIAM. No. Does it make any difference?
ANN. No, of course not.
WILLIAM. Quite so. I say blackmail because it's as likely as anything else. Well, I play for time. Pour you out a whisky—*the* whisky—and while you're sipping it, I cross casually to the fireplace, keeping up a brisk conversation—take the poker—and poke the dying fire.
ANN. It's never been lit.
WILLIAM. Very well, I don't poke the fire. I toy with the ornaments.
ANN. There aren't any.
WILLIAM. I pick up the poker or whatever else is handy. Quietly I approach the sofa from the back.
ANN (*suddenly picking up Reginald's envelope from the sofa*) Oh, he's left it behind.
WILLIAM. What?
ANN. Reginald. He's left the manuscript of his poem here.
WILLIAM (*annoyed at being interrupted*) What of it? Quietly I approach the sofa from behind . . .
ANN. But he was going to read it tonight on the Third Programme.
WILLIAM. He's bound to have another copy. Quietly I approach . . .
ANN. I don't think he has.
WILLIAM. He's probably learnt it by heart.
ANN. He can't have done. It's a modern poem.
WILLIAM. Then he can make it up as he goes along. Please pay attention. This is really important. The more I think about it the simpler it becomes. All this time I've been getting nearer, suddenly I lean over and with the other hand——
ANN. But I'm sure Regin——
WILLIAM. —stifle your screams—and before you can utter a sound I give you a violent blow with a blunt instrument. You struggle, but I have my hand over your mouth. (*He grabs her mouth with one hand*)

   (ANN, *taken completely by surprise, and in wild alarm, thrusts out her hands and seizes William by the throat.* WILLIAM *tries so desperately to free himself that they roll off the sofa on to the floor.*
   REGINALD *lets himself in by the front door and crosses hurriedly to the sofa. He stops abruptly as he sees* ANN *and* WILLIAM *rolling on the floor. They both look up and see Reginald*)

REGINALD. Ann!
ANN (*lamely*) Oh, Reginald, I found your poem.
REGINALD (*in a terribly strained voice*) What are you doing on the floor with that fellow?

WILLIAM (*getting to his feet*) Waiting for the police. (*He assists* ANN *to get to her feet*)
REGINALD. Do you expect me to believe that?
WILLIAM. I was simply conducting an experiment with your fiancée.
REGINALD. I'm not interested in the preliminaries.
ANN. Listen to me, Reginald. (*To William*) And you shut up.
REGINALD. I refuse to listen.
ANN. Reginald, someone's been murdered—the body is here in this room.
REGINALD. I beg your pardon?
ANN. It's in the piano.
REGINALD. Ann, what on earth *has* come over you?
ANN (*frantically*) I tell you there's a body in the piano.
REGINALD. What?
ANN (*excitedly*) It's a woman, Reginald. She was battered from behind with her mouth shut.

(REGINALD *crosses swiftly to the piano*)

(*She turns away*) Reginald! Don't. (*She covers her face with her hands*)

(REGINALD *ignores Ann, lifts the lid of the piano, peers inside, then closes the lid and turns to stare at William*)

REGINALD (*after a pause*) I suppose you think that's funny?
WILLIAM. Eh? (*He crosses to the piano, lifts the lid and looks inside*)
ANN (*turning*) What's happened?
WILLIAM. I tell you, she was there when I left the room.

(ANN *crosses to the piano, lifts the lid and peers inside*)

ANN (*bewildered*) There's nothing there.
WILLIAM. But it's incredible. Somebody must have moved her. I struck B flat and it wasn't there. (*He strikes the note two or three times and it plays correctly*) Now—it's there, and she isn't.
REGINALD (*crossing to* C; *to Ann*) What you can hope to gain by this ludicrous charade, I can't think.
WILLIAM (*lamely*) It isn't a charade.
REGINALD. I was not addressing you. (*To Ann*) It's absolutely beyond me how you could bring yourself to listen to the demented vaporizings of this common adventurer.
WILLIAM. I beg your pardon, Charterhouse, and—well, never mind.
REGINALD (*ignoring William*) I can only say, Ann, that you've shown me a side to your nature which I never dreamed existed.
ANN (*crossing to* R *of Reginald; recovering her spirit*) How dare you talk to me like that in front of a stranger!
REGINALD. Stranger. Huh!
WILLIAM. Not so much of the "huh"!

REGINALD (*turning to William*) Be silent, sir. I enter my house...
ANN. *Your* house!
REGINALD. Certainly it's my house.
WILLIAM. Who paid the deposit?
REGINALD (*turning to face Ann*) I enter my house to discover you alone with that fellow, hiding for some obscure reason behind the sofa. Later I come back to find the position has deteriorated to the point where you are rolling on the floor with him in your underwear...
ANN (*interrupting; furiously*) If you say another word, I'll smack your face.
REGINALD. Should I be so foolish as to return yet again, I shudder to think...

(ANN *smacks Reginald's face.* REGINALD *stares at her for a full second, then grabs his hat and jams it on his head. Unfortunately, it is the bowler hat left by Montague*)

This is the end of the chapter.

(REGINALD *exits by the front door, slamming it after him*)

WILLIAM (*looking admiringly at Ann*) You were magnificent. Absolutely magnificent.
ANN (*rounding on him*) You dirty, lying hound!
WILLIAM. Eh?
ANN (*shouting*) Clear out and leave me alone. (*She throws herself on the sofa*) Oh, why did I believe such a damned silly story?
WILLIAM (*perching himself on the left arm of the sofa; sympathetically*) But it's true. It really is true.
ANN. Don't come near me.
WILLIAM. But I did see it.
ANN. You didn't.
WILLIAM. I did. I tell you I saw a woman's arm. I touched it.

(REGINALD *rushes in by the front door, bangs Montague's hat on the table, picks up his own hat, jams it on his head, then turns to William and Ann*)

REGINALD. My poem.
WILLIAM (*to Ann*) His poem.
REGINALD (*fiercely*) I want it.
WILLIAM. He wants it.

(ANN *feels for the poem and drags it out from underneath her*)

ANN (*savagely*) Take it. (*She passes the poem to William*)
WILLIAM (*handing the poem to Reginald*) I pass.
REGINALD (*moving close to William; between his teeth*) By heaven, I'd give you the thrashing of your life——

(WILLIAM *rises*)

—if I didn't have to read the nine o'clock news.

(REGINALD *exits angrily, leaving the front door ajar*)

WILLIAM. Pity to let him go like that. The weather forecast tonight will be terrible.

ANN. If he was half a man he'd have given you a good hiding instead of just talking about it.

WILLIAM. I suppose it's hopeless to try and convince you?

ANN. Absolutely.

WILLIAM. I thought so. I'm beginning to wonder if I ought not to doubt it myself.

ANN (*sarcastically*) Are you really? How remarkable.

WILLIAM. Yet I know I touched her arm. She was wearing a black dress.

ANN (*rising*) And she felt so uncomfortable in the piano that she got up and went home.

WILLIAM. Why should I tell you I saw her there if I didn't?

ANN (*slowly*) Wait a minute. Didn't you say you phoned the police?

WILLIAM. Yes.

ANN (*sharply*) Then why aren't they here? When someone reports a murder they don't hang about, do they?

WILLIAM. By jove, you're right. Why *aren't* they here?

ANN. Because you never phoned them, of course.

WILLIAM. No—now I come to think of it, I didn't.

ANN. You didn't?

WILLIAM. No. The fellow next door did. I—I wonder . . .

ANN. What?

WILLIAM (*thinking aloud*) Of course he didn't. (*He crosses to the window*) He only pretended to make that call. Don't you see . . .

ANN (*interrupting*) I'm afraid I don't see. I'm going to change now, and if you haven't removed yourself when I come back——

(WILLIAM *stares out of the window*)

—I shall phone the police myself and have you thrown out.

(*The front door swings slowly open.*
    WINIFRED *enters by the front door and staggers slowly* C. *She wears a black dress. She is in a complete daze. Across her forehead is a streak of blood.* ANN *lets out a shriek*)

WILLIAM. What's the matter? (*He turns, sees Winifred staggering, rushes forward and catches her as she collapses in a heap*) Quick—some brandy! (*He lifts her bodily and places her on the sofa*)

ANN (*recovering her nerve*) We haven't any.

WILLIAM. Whisky, then—anything. (*He points to the table up* RC) That bottle.

(ANN *moves hurriedly to the table, picks up the bottle and a glass, tips the bottle but only a few drops come out*)

ANN. There's only a drop.

WILLIAM. Right. Pity there isn't more—we could all do with a shot.

ANN (*moving below the sofa*) Is she the . . . ? (*She looks fearfully towards the piano*)

WILLIAM. Yes.

ANN (*handing the glass to William*) Then she's not dead.

WILLIAM (*holding the glass to Winifred's mouth*) Well—she *wasn't* when she came in the door. Wait a minute—no, she's definitely swallowing.

ANN. Oh! We shouldn't have given it to her.

WILLIAM. What?

ANN. The whisky.

WILLIAM. Why not?

ANN. Not in cases of shock.

WILLIAM. Why didn't you think of that before?

ANN. Well, you used to be a medical student.

(WINIFRED *opens her eyes*)

WILLIAM. She's coming round. (*He helps Winifred into a sitting position*)

WINIFRED. W-what—where . . . ?

WILLIAM. There—there—you're quite safe.

ANN. Ask her how she got in the piano.

WILLIAM. Give her a chance.

WINIFRED (*suddenly clutching desperately at William*) You've got to—stop them.

WILLIAM. Stop who?

WINIFRED. Sir Gregory—we must warn him.

ANN. Sir Gregory?

WINIFRED. Upshott—Sir Gregory Upshott—I work for him. (*Tensely*) The time—quick—what's the time?

ANN. It must be nearly nine.

WINIFRED (*struggling to her feet; wildly*) Ten forty-eight—it will happen at ten forty-eight—hurry. (*She collapses and falls over William's shoulder*)

WILLIAM (*putting Winifred on the sofa*) She's fainted. (*He gives her some more whisky*)

(WINIFRED *opens her eyes*)

Tell us—what's going to happen at ten forty-eight?

WINIFRED. Eh? They're going to kill him.

ANN (*to William*) We *must* send for the police.

WINIFRED (*fiercely*) No—there's no time. They won't believe it —and he's using another name. (*She clutches at William*) It's going to go off at ten forty-eight.

WILLIAM. What?

(WINIFRED *faints*)

She's out again. (*He bends over her*) Listen . . .

(*There is no response*)

(*To Ann*) You know who Sir Gregory Upshott is, don't you?

ANN. Isn't he something to do with the Government?

WILLIAM. Yes—he's the special envoy we always send out East every time our oil's going west. (*He shakes Winifred*) Listen to me, you must tell us what this is all about.

(WILLIAM *energetically shakes* WINIFRED, *who murmurs, half raises her hand, passes it over her forehead and stares at William*)

WINIFRED (*in a flat, strained voice*) ". . . the moment of impact may not be far ahead . . . disappear, this time finally, from the public scene."

WILLIAM. Eh?

(MONTAGUE *enters by the front door. He is unseen by the others. He holds Hawkins' ancient revolver in one hand, and a chloroform pad in the other. He stealthily approaches the group at the sofa.* WINIFRED *slowly pushes William aside and sits bolt upright, her stare curiously blank.* ANN *and* WILLIAM *look blankly at each other*)

WINIFRED (*seizing William's arm*) That's when don't you see? Somebody must warn him. They know he's going to the coast.

(MONTAGUE *moves behind the sofa*)

They know it's the *Green Man* at New——

(MONTAGUE *suddenly presses the chloroform pad over Winifred's mouth, speaking rapidly at the same time*)

MONTAGUE (*to William and Ann*) Get back over there.

WILLIAM (*recognizing him*) Oh—hello. (*To Ann*) Mr Bostock.

MONTAGUE. Keep your mouth shut. (*He waves them back with the revolver*)

(WILLIAM *does not move and* ANN *stays by his side*)

WILLIAM. Would you mind explaining what the hell is going on?

MONTAGUE. I warn you—I'm not in a mood to stand any nonsense. One squawk out of either of you and you've had it.

WILLIAM (*to Ann*) An unoriginal type, I'm afraid.

MONTAGUE. I said— shut your mouth!

(WILLIAM *suddenly looks up with bright surprise towards the front door*)

WILLIAM (*conversationally*) Oh, hello, Reginald, old boy—come in.

(MONTAGUE *involuntarily looks round at the front door, though the revolver still points directly at* WILLIAM, *who shakes Ann free and takes a flying leap at* MONTAGUE. *They go down in a heap behind the sofa, out of sight. There is the sound of a violent struggle, then* WILLIAM'S *head appears momentarily above the sofa*)

The bottle!

(MONTAGUE'S *hand grabs* WILLIAM'S *hair, and pulls him out of sight*)

(*He pops his head up again*) The bottle!

(ANN *moves to the table up* RC *and picks up the whisky bottle.* MONTAGUE *grabs* WILLIAM *and he disappears with a jerk. There are sounds of violence, then a hand appears.* ANN *puts the whisky bottle in it, it is swept down and followed by a thud*)

(*He rises slowly, bottle in hand, much dishevelled*) Oh, well—we got a double out of it after all. (*He removes the pad from Winifred's mouth, sniffs it and reacts*) Chloroform. Well, this is a fine state of affairs. (*He puts the pad on the table*)

ANN. I wonder what she meant?

WILLIAM. We might persuade him to tell us—if he comes round.

ANN. No, no. This time we really *must* call the police.

WILLIAM. And tell them what?

ANN. That somebody is after Sir Gregory. Remember what she said—". . . the moment of impact might not be far ahead."

WILLIAM. And something or other is going off at ten forty-eight?

ANN. That's right.

WILLIAM. Can you imagine the reaction of the average copper if we told him *that*? We'd spend the night in the looney-bin. (*He picks up his hat and crosses to the front door*)

ANN. Where are you going?

WILLIAM. I'm driving down there in my car.

ANN. Where?

WILLIAM. To the place she said. The *Green Man* at New——

ANN. New?

WILLIAM. New? Yes, that's a point.

ANN. That's what I was thinking.

WILLIAM. What we need is a map.

ANN. I think there's an A.A. book of Reginald's somewhere. (*She crosses to the packing case* L, *and searches in it for the book*)

WILLIAM. That'll do if you can find one.

ANN (*searching*) The *Green Man* may not have meant a thing—she was half delirious.

WILLIAM. We'll have to chance that. She said something about the coast, so New-whatever it is must be somewhere on the coast.

And she seemed to think there was time to get down there by ten forty-eight.

ANN (*taking an A.A. handbook from the case*) Here's one.

WILLIAM (*perching himself on the left arm of the easy chair*) Give it to me—let's see what "News" there are.

ANN (*sitting on the packing case* L *of William and peering over his shoulder*) New Brighton.

WILLIAM. That's in Cheshire.

ANN. Newbury.

WILLIAM. *That's* not on the coast—and New York's in America —so that leaves Newcliffe and Newhaven, and that's the end of the "News". Wait a minute—Newcliffe—(*he reads*) "London fifty-five miles. The *Green Man*, twelve stars, two beds." I mean twelve beds, two stars.

ANN (*pointing to another entry in the book*) What about Newhaven? They've got a *Green Man*, too.

WILLIAM. Newhaven is simply a port. Newcliffe is a health resort.

ANN. Well, it doesn't sound as if it will be very healthy there tonight—that is if it is Newcliffe.

WILLIAM (*putting the book on the piano*) Fifty-five miles. (*He rises*) I ought to do it easily in an hour and a half. (*He crosses to* C)

ANN (*rising*) What about these two? (*She crosses to* L *of William*) We can't leave her with him—he might come round first.

WILLIAM. Soon settle that. (*He picks up the pad, sniffs it and recoils, then drops the pad on to Montague's face*) Sleep well. (*He glances at Winifred*) She won't be round for at least an hour. (*To Ann*) Now then—have you got any rope?

ANN. No.

WILLIAM. Anything then, string—picture cord.

ANN (*looking around*) Yes—picture cord. (*She crosses to the piano and picks up the cord from Reginald's package*) Of course, I still think it's Newhaven. (*She crosses and hands the cord to William*)

WILLIAM (*raising Montague's feet*) Well, I'm not going there. (*He starts to tie Montague's feet and gets the cord around Ann's waist*)

ANN. Ouch! That's *me*!

WILLIAM (*withdrawing the cord*) At one time I used to be a Sea Scout—and to be a Sea Scout you have to know how to tie a sheepshank, a fisherman's bend, a bowline and—an old-fashioned granny. (*He ties Montague's feet*) Which is the only one I remember. (*He lets Montague's feet drop with a thud, then ties his hands*)

ANN. I'm going to change.

(ANN *exits hurriedly* R. *The ensuing conversation is carried on in shouts,* ANN *from off* R, *and* WILLIAM *from behind the sofa*)

WILLIAM. Why?

ANN (*off*) I'm coming with you.

WILLIAM. Oh, no, you're not.
ANN (*off*) You're taking me.
WILLIAM. I'm not taking any woman on a trip like this.
ANN (*off*) There's no danger till a quarter to eleven—she said so.
WILLIAM (*satirically*) Of course, so far it's been roses, roses all the way.
ANN (*off*) We're both still here, aren't we?
WILLIAM. Yes. And that's where you're staying. (*He rises and stands behind the sofa*) That ought to hold him for a bit—even my old skipper couldn't untie my knots—that's why I left the sea.
ANN (*off*) What about her?
WILLIAM. I was just thinking about her. (*He moves below the sofa*) I'll make her a bit more comfortable. (*He settles Winifred comfortably on the sofa*)

(ANN *enters* R. *She is now fully dressed*)

(*He looks admiringly at Ann*) I say! If ever I get hitched up I hope she changes as quickly as you do.
ANN (*slightly confused by this*) I didn't want you to go without me. (*She crosses to* C)
WILLIAM (*moving to* R *of Ann*) But I am.
ANN. You're not.
WILLIAM. Listen—even if her story is fifty per cent nonsense, we've certainly no time to stand here arguing. Besides, what would Reginald say?
ANN (*giving him a funny look*) I'd forgotten all about him.
WILLIAM. You couldn't do better. I'm sorry, I shouldn't have said that. Good-bye. (*He moves to the front door*)
ANN. Please wait. (*She hurries to the window seat and pulls out a telephone from behind the upstage window-curtain*)
WILLIAM (*stopping and turning*) I say—you've got a *phone*.
ANN. Yes. (*She lifts the receiver and dials a number*)
WILLIAM. And you haven't moved in yet! I've been on the waiting list for one of those for two and half years.
ANN. Reginald naturally has priority.
WILLIAM (*under his breath*) Reginald has . . .
ANN (*into the telephone*) B.B.C.? . . . Extension thirty-seven A . . . Mr Willoughby-Pratt, please. (*She waits*)
WILLIAM. *He's* not coming. That's definite.
ANN. It's only fair to tell him where we're going.
WILLIAM. Have you a watch?
ANN. Not with me.
WILLIAM. That's awkward. Not even an alarm clock?
ANN. No. (*She nods towards Winifred*) What are you going to do with her?
WILLIAM. She'll be a nice surprise for Reginald.

ANN (*into the telephone*) Reginald? ... This is Ann ... Listen, Reginald ... But I *haven't* rung you up to apologize ... I've something much more important to tell you. Reginald, there *was* a body in the piano ... I know, but it came back ... I'm not being absurd. Listen! It's terribly serious, and I'm going down to the *Green Man* at Newcliffe with Mr Blake ... Of course, we'll be alone, but what's that got to do with it? ... Reginald! (*She turns furiously to William*) He's rung off! (*She replaces the receiver*)

WILLIAM. Good.

ANN. I won't tell you what he said.

WILLIAM. I got the gist.

ANN. How *dare* he?

WILLIAM. Well, I think that settles the question. (*He turns towards the front door*) Wish me luck.

ANN. Do you think I'd stay here after *that*? I'm ready. Come on, let's go.

WILLIAM. Can I ask you a personal question?

ANN. What?

WILLIAM. Why this sudden faith in me?

ANN. Well, it looks as if you were right after all.

WILLIAM. It's taken two bodies to prove it.

ANN. Besides, to be absolutely frank—well, any man who can attack someone who's pointing a loaded revolver at him has guts.

WILLIAM (*picking up the revolver from the floor above the sofa*) I'm sorry to disillusion you, but *this*—(*he holds up the revolver*) was offered to me by your next door neighbour and he assured me it wasn't loaded.

ANN. That's the last thing I expected of you.

WILLIAM. What?

ANN. Modesty.

WILLIAM. You don't believe me?

ANN. Of course not.

WILLIAM. 'Tis true, 'tis pity and pity 'tis, 'tis true!

(WILLIAM *points the revolver at the ceiling, presses the trigger and the gun goes off with a loud report*)

CURTAIN

To face page 45 *Meet A Body* *Photograph by Houston Rogers*

ACT III

SCENE—*The Bar Parlour of the "Green Man", Newcliffe. The same night.*

The "Green Man" is a small eighteenth-century hotel standing on the cliffs of the Sussex coast. It is very prosperous in its way, doing a fair amount from weekenders. The parlour has an arch back c leading to the entrance hall and other bars. A door L leads to the dining-room. There is an alcove LC with a staircase leading up and off L to the bedrooms. The fireplace is R and there are french windows up R opening on to a balcony with a concrete balustrade. The window overlooks the cliff edge, and in the distance is a view of the sea with the lights of Brighton pier in the distance. Between the arch c and the staircase alcove there is a small serving hatch with a shutter. In front of the fireplace is a wicker settee, a small table and a wicker armchair. A similar wicker table with two upright wicker chairs stands LC. A large radiogram on which is a small white portable radio receiver stands against the staircase. There is a large gong with a framed menu above the door L. A grandfather clock stands in a corner of the staircase. Under the serving hatch is a small table with a telephone. In the downstage corner of the window is a built-in seat. The walls are decorated with sporting prints and at night the parlour is lit by swan-neck electric brackets, two over the fireplace and one each on the staircase and over the door L. The hall beyond the arch c is furnished with a hall-stand. There are the usual advertisements of beers and spirits, and a stuffed fish in a glass case hangs over the mirror above the mantelpiece.

(See the Ground Plan and Photograph of the scene)

When the CURTAIN *rises, the grandfather clock stands at ten-twenty. The lights are on and the french windows stand open.* CHARLES BOUGHT-FLOWER *is standing down* RC *earnestly checking several pieces of paper, one with another. He is a stoutish, middle-aged man in tweeds. The* LANDLORD, *a tall lank figure in the middle fifties, enters from the hall. He is followed on by* HAWKINS, *who is wearing his overcoat, and carrying his attaché-case. He puts the case on the floor by the hall-stand, removes his overcoat and hangs it on the hall-stand as he comes in.*

LANDLORD (*as he enters*) This way, sir. This is the lounge. If you care to glance out of the window here Brightonwards, you can see the lights of the pier. Right on the edge of the cliffs we are here, sir. As a matter of fact this balcony's famous in a way, a gentleman threw himself off of it last year. Doctor he was—left a note saying he was taking the quickest way out of the health service.

HAWKINS (*moving* c) Really, I quite sympathize with him. Let me see, what's the time? (*He glances at his watch*) If I have a little supper—you say it's ready?

LANDLORD. Yes, sir. It's cold, I'm afraid.

HAWKINS. Never mind. I suppose I can have a drink?

LANDLORD. 'Fraid not, sir. Bar closed at ten. Unless you're staying the night.

HAWKINS. No—er—I don't exactly anticipate that. Never mind, a cup of cocoa will do.

LANDLORD. Very good, sir. (*He crosses and rings the bell push above the fireplace. To* BOUGHTFLOWER) Good evening, Mr Boughtflower. How's Wardour Street? Sold any good films lately?

BOUGHTFLOWER. I'm selling them in assorted sizes nowadays—wide, wider and blooming enormous. I tell you, I'm flogging Jane Russell at so much an acre.

LANDLORD (*crossing to* RC) Ah—checking your pools?

BOUGHTFLOWER (*grunting*) Umm!

LANDLORD. Anywhere near this week?

BOUGHTFLOWER (*shaking his head*) I'm all right on my ones and twos but my draws have let me down.

> (HAWKINS *glances at the portable radio receiver with interest and crosses to it.*
> LILY, *a buxom barmaid in the early thirties, enters up* C)

LILY. Did you ring, sir?

LANDLORD. Yes, Lily. Tell Tucker to get supper for this gentleman and a cup of cocoa.

LILY. O.K.

> (LILY *exits up* C. *The* LANDLORD *notices* HAWKINS *examining the radio*)

LANDLORD. Interested in wireless, sir?

HAWKINS. Er—yes, it's a hobby of mine, in a way.

LANDLORD (*proudly*) That's the last word in transportables, they tell me. Chap came round yesterday with it—said I could have it for a month on trial free—and if at the end I don't want it, he'll take it back without charging a penny.

HAWKINS. That sounds fair enough.

BOUGHTFLOWER. I'd let him have it back. It crackles.

HAWKINS. Probably some minor fault, you know, such things are easily put right.

> (LILY *enters up* C)

LILY (*to the Landlord*) Lady and gentlemen waiting to see you in the hall. Say they've booked.

LANDLORD. Ah, yes. That'll be the couple for the big double. (*To* HAWKINS) The dining-room's in there, sir. (*He points to the door* L)

HAWKINS. Thank you.

(HAWKINS *crosses and exits* L.

The LANDLORD *exits up* C. LILY *looks to see that the coast is clear, then turns to Boughtflower*)

LILY (*crossing to the fireplace*) Had you any difficulty getting away, Charlie? (*She collects two dirty glasses from the mantelpiece*)

BOUGHTFLOWER. Like hell I did. We've got to be much more careful. My wife's beginning to tumble.

LILY. I knew that was coming. (*She crosses and puts the glasses on the shelf of the hatch*)

BOUGHTFLOWER. Keeps dropping hints—harping on a friend of hers who's bringing an action for enticement.

LILY. You'll have to watch your step, Charlie, I don't want any trouble. The Guvnor wouldn't mind, but the brewers would.

BOUGHTFLOWER. You know, it's me being away weekends, puts ideas in her head.

LILY (*crossing to* L *of him*) Your wife doesn't expect you to sell films sitting at home, does she?

BOUGHTFLOWER. That's what I tell her. If you've got *The Robe* or Marilyn Monroe you can afford to sit on your backside—but what have I got?

LILY (*putting her arms around his neck*) You've got everything, Charlie.

BOUGHTFLOWER (*grinning admiringly at her*) Well, I'm not the only one.

LILY. Still, you'll have to be more careful. You don't want her following you, or any of that caper.

BOUGHTFLOWER (*disengaging himself*) Don't you worry. I've laid me red herrings all right. I'm supposed to be staying in Walton-on-the-Naze this week-end. (*He crosses up* C) Now, which room have I got? I'd like to have a wash. (*He picks up his case from beside the hatch*)

LILY. Single on the top floor, next the Guvnor's.

BOUGHTFLOWER (*grinning*) I hope the floor boards don't creak.

LILY. They do, but I've marked the creakers with bits of paper.

BOUGHTFLOWER. Think of everything, don't you? O.K., kid.

(BOUGHTFLOWER *exits up the stairs.*

The LANDLORD, SIR GREGORY UPSHOTT *and* JOAN WOOD *enter up* C. SIR GREGORY *is stoutish and bald. He wears an overcoat and cap.* JOAN *is a pretty but very nervous and self-conscious girl in her twenties*)

LANDLORD (*as he enters*) This way, sir. This is the lounge. I've reserved a double room for you at the front. It's got a nice outlook facing the sea, just above this one.

(LILY *exits up* C. JOAN *stands nervously-down* RC)

SIR GREGORY (*crossing to* C) Splendid.

LANDLORD. If you care to glance out of the window here, Brightonwards, madam, you'll see the lights of the pier.

SIR GREGORY. There's a bath, I take it?

LANDLORD. Just across the landing, sir.

SIR GREGORY (*displeased*) Oh, I see. Hot and cold water, I hope? (*He removes his cap, puts it on the table* LC, *then takes off his overcoat*)

LANDLORD. Well, sir, Saturday night there's a bit of a run, but I'll have the boiler stoked up for you.

SIR GREGORY (*even more put out*) We're not too late for supper by any chance?

LANDLORD (*taking the coat from Sir Gregory*) No, sir. But I'm afraid it's cold.

SIR GREGORY. Really! You know, you fellows will have to smarten up your ideas a bit. You won't capture the foreign tourists this way.

LANDLORD (*hanging the coat on the hall-stand*) I don't want to capture no foreigners, sir. I'm quite happy with my weekend customers, thanks all the same.

SIR GREGORY. Oh! (*He coughs*) Hrrm! All right, we'll have to have it cold.

LANDLORD. Yes, sir. Something to drink first, sir?

SIR GREGORY. Drink? Oh, yes, I'll have a whisky and soda. (*To Joan*) What about you, my dear?

JOAN. I don't want anything, thank you very much.

(*The* LANDLORD *moves to the hatch and knocks on it*)

SIR GREGORY. Oh, come, you can't let me drink alone. (*He crosses to* L *of Joan*) How about a bottle of champagne?

JOAN (*intimidated*) Champagne?

SIR GREGORY (*to the Landlord*) Have you got any?

LANDLORD. I think so, sir.

SIR GREGORY. Any Pol Roger?

LANDLORD (*cautiously*) I don't remember the name, sir, but I'm as good as certain it's French.

(LILY *opens the hatch from behind and takes in the empty glasses*)

SIR GREGORY (*giving it up*) Oh, all right. Bring it.

LANDLORD. Would you care to see the room first?

(LILY *closes the hatch*)

SIR GREGORY. The room? Oh yes, of course, the room. (*To Joan*) Come along, my dear.

(*The* LANDLORD *moves to the foot of the stairs*)

JOAN (*nervously tugging at Sir Gregory's sleeve*) Not now.

SIR GREGORY. What?

JOAN. I'd rather stay here, if it's all the same to you, sir.

Sir Gregory. Oh. (*He coughs*) Very well. As you please. We'll see the room later, landlord.

Landlord (*crossing to the arch up* c) Yes, sir. Perhaps you wouldn't mind signing the register while I order supper.

Sir Gregory. The register, oh, yes. Quite so.

(*The* Landlord *collects the register from the hall-stand, crosses and puts it on the table* LC)

Landlord. Here you are, sir. (*He points to the door* L) The dining-room's in there, sir. I'll have your luggage sent up.

(*The* Landlord *exits up* C. Sir Gregory *watches him go then turns to Joan*)

Sir Gregory. My dear Joan, you really must try to appear more at ease.

Joan. I don't feel at ease.

Sir Gregory. Do you realize you called me "sir" just now?

Joan. Oh, did I? I'm afraid, Sir Gregory. (*She crosses and sits on the chair* R *of the table* LC)

Sir Gregory (*crossing and standing above the table* LC) There's no need to call me that. Just "Gregory" now. What are you afraid of?

Joan. I know someone will recognize you.

Sir Gregory. Of course they won't without my moustache.

Joan. You look just the same to me.

Sir Gregory. That's only because you know me.

Joan. What about the cartoons?

Sir Gregory. Nothing like me at all.

Joan. You can't alter your bald head. Everyone knows that.

Sir Gregory (*picking up his cap and putting it on*) Just to please you I'll put my cap on.

(Joan *takes one look at him and bursts into tears*)

What's the matter?

Joan. You can't keep it on all the time.

Sir Gregory. Now please, Joan, don't be fanciful. No-one will look at us or bother about us in the least. Just try to forget convention and look upon this as an adventure—a gay adventure. After all, what *is* convention? I've travelled a lot and I can tell you it changes with the latitude. The Moslems, for instance, have a totally different attitude to latitude. (*He laughs, delighted with his joke*) I'm really excelling myself this evening.

Joan (*flatly*) Mother's not a Moslem.

(Sir Gregory's *smile fades abruptly*)

Sir Gregory. I do wish you wouldn't keep on about your mother. Does she have to be brought into everything?

Joan. I don't want her brought into this.

SIR GREGORY. You know, you've been the same ever since we left. You're not the little girl I knew in London, that I used to take out for those cosy little dinners in Charlotte Street.

JOAN. This isn't a cosy little dinner in Charlotte Street.

SIR GREGORY. Now you don't want me to wish I hadn't brought you away.

JOAN. I didn't want to come, anyway.

SIR GREGORY. What?

JOAN. It was only because you kept on at me.

SIR GREGORY. I don't know how you can say that, Joan. You know I'm very fond of you and I've done everything I could to please you.

JOAN. Just because you promised to put me in Grade One ...

SIR GREGORY. That was quite unconnected with this trip. Didn't I tell you I wanted to encourage you to be ambitious—take responsibility—get more experience—

JOAN. —broaden my mind?

SIR GREGORY. That's right. (*He coughs. Hurriedly*) Now do please try to pull yourself together and no more inhibitions, eh? (*He opens the register*) Now let's see if we can think of something original to write in this book, shall we? Any ideas?

(JOAN *shakes her head*)

Extraordinary how one's mind becomes a blank with all the names in Christendom to choose from. Hmm, let's think of a famous writer. What about Reade—Charles Reade?

JOAN. I've never heard of him.

SIR GREGORY. Famous novelist, my dear—he wrote *It's Never Too Late to Mend*. (*Suddenly realizing the implication*) Well, nobody reads him nowadays. How about Fothrington?

JOAN. It doesn't sound real.

SIR GREGORY. But it is. I once knew a horse called Fothrington. Wait a minute, though, we can't use that.

JOAN. Why not?

SIR GREGORY. I've just remembered I must have put a name on the telegram I sent here.

JOAN (*rising; alarmed*) Don't you know what it was?

SIR GREGORY. Hmm, must have put something. James, that was it, James.

(JOAN *suddenly bursts into tears*)

Now what on earth's the trouble this time?

JOAN (*crying*) I used to be engaged to a boy called James.

(HAWKINS *enters* L *and pulls up short on seeing Sir Gregory and Joan.* SIR GREGORY, *seeing Hawkins, becomes a little confused*)

SIR GREGORY (*to Joan*) Now, now, my dear, don't cry, you probably left the watch in the car. You haven't lost it yet.

(HAWKINS *crosses to the hall-stand, fumbles in his coat pocket and takes out a bottle of digestive tablets*)

JOAN (*dumbly*) Haven't lost what?

(SIR GREGORY, *confused, bustles* JOAN *off* L. HAWKINS *watches them go, then takes a quick look into the hall, picks up his attaché-case and crosses swiftly to the radio on top of the radiogram. Opening his attaché-case, he takes out a short length of flex, a pair of pliers and a small screwdriver. He then swivels round the radio and opens its back and deftly connects the flex to a couple of terminals. He glances at both his watch and the grandfather clock and makes a swift adjustment with his screwdriver.*

BOUGHTFLOWER *enters and stands on the stairs, looking down curiously at Hawkins*)

BOUGHTFLOWER. Trying to fix that crackle?

(HAWKINS, *surprised, looks up, but quickly takes advantage of Boughtflower's words*)

HAWKINS. Ah, yes, I told you wireless was a hobby of mine. (*He laughs*) I'm afraid I'm one of those people who can't see any mechanism without wanting to tinker with it. I expect you've met them. (*He gives a careful last look inside the radio, closes it, then puts his tools in the attaché-case and stands it beside the radiogram*)

BOUGHTFLOWER (*nodding as he comes downstairs*) The wife's father's just the same. Can't keep his hands off the television. Result is, we see everything through a rainstorm.

HAWKINS. Yes, I know. (*He turns the radio to face front*) Sometimes fellows like he and I make the whole place quite untenable—in one way or another. (*He switches on the radio*)

(*The radio warms up and dance music is heard*)

Doesn't seem to be much crackle about that.

BOUGHTFLOWER. It certainly sounds better. Finished your supper already?

HAWKINS. No. I came back to get my indigestion tablets, really.

BOUGHTFLOWER. It's usually that sort of supper here. (*He crosses to the window*) Still, you can't have everything, can you? If you look Brightonwards you can see the lights of the pier.

HAWKINS (*switching off the radio*) So I gathered. Well, back to the feast—cold rabbit pie and cocoa. I'll see you later perhaps.

BOUGHTFLOWER. Yes. I'll still be here.

HAWKINS (*dryly*) I hope so.

(HAWKINS *crosses and exits* L. BOUGHTFLOWER *steps out on to the balcony.*
LILY, WILLIAM *and* ANN *enter up* C)

LILY. If you don't mind waiting here, sir, I'll fetch the Guvnor.

(WILLIAM *glances quickly around the room and spots the grandfather clock, which now stands at ten twenty-seven*)

WILLIAM. Is that clock right?
LILY. It's always right Saturday night, sir.
ANN. Why Saturday?
LILY. Well, you see, it loses ten minutes a week, so the Guvnor puts it on ten minutes every Saturday and by the end of the week it's back with Big Ben, so to speak.
WILLIAM. So long as you're sure that's the right time.
LILY (*glancing at her watch*) Bang on, sir.

(LILY *exits up* C)

WILLIAM (*at once becoming active*) It won't be the only thing that's bang on if we don't get cracking. We've exactly twenty-one minutes.
ANN. What are you going to do?
WILLIAM. Have a look at the register.
ANN. What about telling the landlord?
WILLIAM. Let's see if Upshott's here first.
LILY (*off*) They're in the parlour, Mr Masters.

(*The* LANDLORD *enters up* C)

LANDLORD. Evening, sir.
WILLIAM. Good evening.
LANDLORD. Evening, madam. Lovely night. If you're wanting a double room I'm afraid we haven't one left. It's always a bit of a rush weekends this time of the year.
WILLIAM. Have you any singles?
LANDLORD. I've only one free, sir. Bit on the small side, too.
WILLIAM. Oh. Suppose we'll have to manage with that. (*To Ann*) Won't we, my dear?

(ANN *chokes and starts to speak*)

(*He quickly fixes her with a look*) I know it's a bit of a blow, but there's nothing else for it. (*He winks at her*)
LANDLORD. Mind you, the bed's on the big side for a single. There's a nice outlook. If you care to glance out of the window, Brightonwards, you'll see the lights of the pier.
ANN (*suddenly bursting out at William*) If you think . . .
WILLIAM. Please, dear. I know it's a nuisance, but after all I did suggest sending a wire. (*To the Landlord*) Can we have the register?
LANDLORD. Yes, sir. (*He crosses to the table* LC *and indicates the register*) Here you are. Will you be taking supper?
WILLIAM. I don't know yet.
LANDLORD (*pointing to the door* L) The dining-room's in there, sir.

WILLIAM. Thank you.

(*The* LANDLORD *crosses and exits up* C. ANN *instantly rounds on William*)

ANN. How dare you say we're staying the night?
WILLIAM. Quickest way to get the register.
ANN. There was absolutely no need to suggest we were going to—to stop here.
WILLIAM. No-one will stop here if we don't get down to brass tacks. (*He glances at the clock*) Only twenty minutes to find what is going to go off.
ANN. If anything is.
WILLIAM. She said so, didn't she?
ANN. It might have been a figure of speech and it might have been Newhaven.
WILLIAM (*crossing to the door* L, *opening it and taking a quick glance off*) I tell you—(*he closes the door*) this is the place and ten forty-eight is the time.
ANN. Then why not get on with it instead of arguing?
WILLIAM. I . . . (*He controls himself*) All right. (*He moves to the table* LC *and looks through the register*)
ANN (*crossing and peering over William's shoulder*) What are you looking for?
WILLIAM. Upshott.
ANN. She said he was using another name.
WILLIAM. I know, I know. Here we are. (*He reads*) "Mr and Mrs Alec Morrison, Charles Boughtflower, Mr and Mrs John Smith, Mr and Mrs Victor Jones, Mr and Mrs Tom Smith, Mr and Mrs E. Smith, Mr and Mrs F. Smythe . . ." Gosh, that fellow showed imagination!
ANN. All British subjects, but Charles Boughtflower is the only one staying here on his own.
WILLIAM. And that's a fake name in any nationality.
ANN. Unless Sir Gregory *isn't* on his own.
WILLIAM. That's hardly likely. Have you ever seen him?
ANN. No. Have you?
WILLIAM. No. But I'm sure I've seen his photograph in the paper, and my impression is he's at least sixty, fairly tall, bald, and with a grey moustache.
ANN. That's curious, because my impression is quite different.
WILLIAM. Oh—is it?
ANN. I should say he's not more than forty-two or three, dark, clean-shaven and rather stout.
WILLIAM. We can't both be right.
ANN. I wasn't suggesting that for a moment.
WILLIAM. I know it's a lot to ask, but do you think there's a six to four chance of our agreeing to differ?
ANN (*shrugging*) If you like. I don't mind.

WILLIAM. Then I'll go and look for my version. (*He moves towards the arch up* C)

ANN. How?

WILLIAM. By getting the landlord to introduce me to Boughtflower.

ANN. And what do I do?

WILLIAM. Look for whatever it is that's going to go off.

ANN. Where?

WILLIAM. How do I know? Why not start with the clock? That's a popular . . . Wait a minute, he said he was a clockmaker.

ANN. Who?

WILLIAM. Stand back. (*He warily approaches the clock and nerves himself to open the door*)

(*The moment the door opens, the clock loudly strikes the half-hour.* WILLIAM *jumps back as* ANN *gives a little scream*)

(*He signs her to be quiet, puts his head inside the clock case, peers upwards, then withdraws his head*) Looks normal enough to me. My God, look at the time. (*He moves hurriedly to the arch up* C)

ANN. Where else?

WILLIAM (*impatiently*) Anywhere you think. Use your imagination. Under the settee—behind that picture—up the chimney—in the aspidistra. (*He looks at the aspidistra in the corner up* R) Yes, that's an idea—the apidistra. (*He picks up the plant and pulls it out of the pot by the roots, then searches the inside of the pot with the other hand*)

(*The* LANDLORD *enters up* C)

LANDLORD (*as he enters*) Beg pardon, sir, but have you brought any . . . ? (*He stops short, his eyes glued on the aspidistra in William's hand*)

ANN (*to William*) The landlord.

WILLIAM. Nothing doing . . . Eh? (*He sees the Landlord*) We're looking for a man about sixty, bald with a grey moustache . . .

ANN (*quickly*) Dark, clean-shaven, and not more than forty-three.

WILLIAM. It's a matter of national importance.

LANDLORD (*taking the aspidistra and flower-pot from William*) My mother planted that.

(*The* LANDLORD, *mumbling, exits up* C)

WILLIAM. What's the use of talking to a fellow like that? It's a waste of time. Keep on looking. I'll go and find Boughtflower myself.

ANN (*staring towards the french windows*) There's a man out there on the balcony.

WILLIAM. Where?

(ANN *points to the balcony*)

(*He moves close to the window and peers out*) Doesn't look like him. Not in those tweeds.

ANN. It could be. After all, he is in the country.

WILLIAM. By himself, too.

ANN. And smoking a cigar.

(*They stare hopefully at Boughtflower*)

Look out, he's coming in.

WILLIAM. I'd better handle this.

(BOUGHTFLOWER *enters by the french windows*)

Good evening, sir. D'you happen to be Mr Charles Boughtflower?

BOUGHTFLOWER (*startled*) I don't know you, do I?

WILLIAM. No. But we know you, sir.

BOUGHTFLOWER (*at once suspicious*) Eh?

ANN (*to William*) You see, I was right. (*To Boughtflower*) You're here incognito, aren't you?

BOUGHTFLOWER. In—what?

WILLIAM. We've followed you all the way from London.

BOUGHTFLOWER (*alarmed*) Followed me? (*He backs away a step*) What's the idea?

WILLIAM. We've been given certain information . . .

BOUGHTFLOWER. Oh, you have, have you? (*He points to Ann*) Is she with you?

WILLIAM. Yes, but . . .

BOUGHTFLOWER. Two of you, eh?

ANN (*impulsively*) You're not safe here.

BOUGHTFLOWER (*bitterly*) No, you bet your life I'm not. Oh, well, I had this coming to me. (*He sits on the settee*)

ANN. You mean you know all about it?

BOUGHTFLOWER. I had a damned good idea.

WILLIAM (*to Ann*) Well, I suppose it's one of the risks of "Mr Boughtflower's" profession.

(BOUGHTFLOWER *takes this in a big way*)

BOUGHTFLOWER. Risk? (*Cunningly*) What proof have you got, anyway?

WILLIAM. Well, sir, the evidence is pretty conclusive.

BOUGHTFLOWER (*bursting out*) I'm not caught yet, if that's what you mean.

WILLIAM. That's the spirit, sir.

BOUGHTFLOWER (*puzzled*) What?

WILLIAM. Now listen, sir—there's absolutely no time to lose—as I expect you realize. How soon can you get out of here?

BOUGHTFLOWER. Get out?

WILLIAM. You haven't a second.

BOUGHTFLOWER (*narrowing his eyes*) Whose side are you on?

WILLIAM. Need you ask that, sir?

BOUGHTFLOWER. I don't know what you get out of this, but I can take a tip when I'm handed one. (*He rises*) I'll get my case. (*He crosses hurriedly to the stairs*)

WILLIAM. For heaven's sake, hurry!

BOUGHTFLOWER (*going up the stairs*) You bet! (*He pauses briefly half-way and looks over the banisters*) So the old girl thought she'd get me, did she?

(BOUGHTFLOWER *exits hurriedly up the stairs, leaving* WILLIAM *and* ANN *slightly mystified*)

WILLIAM. Old girl? Must be a woman behind it somewhere.

ANN. So it *was* Newcliffe, after all. You win.

WILLIAM. Not yet. We've picked up the ace, but there's still the joker.

ANN. The what?

WILLIAM. The box of tricks. Keep on looking.

ANN. Where are you going?

WILLIAM. We've got to clear everyone out of the whole place. Now we've found Sir Gregory I'll be able to knock some sense into the landlord.

(WILLIAM *exits hurriedly up* C)

ANN (*calling after William*) Oh, Mr Blake—Bill—supposing it goes off too soon. (*She searches frantically round the settee and fireplace*)

(LILY *enters up* C. ANN *runs to the arch up* C *and almost bumps into* LILY, *who stares curiously at her*)

LILY. Your name Vincent?

ANN. Yes.

LILY. There's a man on the phone wants to speak to you. Toll-call.

ANN (*dazed*) A man?

LILY. Sounds like your father. I haven't let on you're here, mind. Like me to tell him there's no-one here of your description?

ANN. No, no—I'll speak to him.

LILY. All right—the phone's through. (*She points to the telephone*)

(ANN *turns to the telephone and lifts the receiver.*
  LILY *exits up* C.
  The LANDLORD *enters up* C. *He carries a plant in a pot*)

ANN (*into the telephone*) Hullo ... Hullo ...

(*The* LANDLORD *sees Ann, sniffs and puts the plant on the stand in the corner up* R)

Who is it? ... *Reginald!* ... Yes, of course I'm here ... Yes, he's here, too ... Reginald! ... Really! ... What *are* you suggesting? ..

(REGINALD *is obviously doing all the talking. The* LANDLORD *has one eye on* ANN, *who has her back to him*)
(*Angrily*) What? . . . I don't know how you can say things like that . . . Do you think we came down here for *fun*? . . .

(*The clock now stands at ten thirty-three*)

What on earth do you mean? . . .

(*The* LANDLORD *gives Ann another look, then takes his watch from his pocket and compares it with the grandfather clock. He crosses to the grandfather clock, and sets the hands on ten minutes so that the clock stands at ten forty-three*)

So you don't believe me? . . . In other words I'm a liar? . . . I tell you I haven't *anything* to conceal . . . I'm not talking to you any longer.

(WILLIAM *enters hurriedly up* C *and hears Ann's last words. The* LANDLORD *stands on the stairs by the grandfather clock*)

I tell you one thing—Mr Blake's got more guts in his little finger . . . Oh, *good*-bye. (*She replaces the receiver*)
WILLIAM (*crossing to* C) Ah, Landlord, there you are. This is important. You remember I asked you about a man just now?
LANDLORD (*moving to* L *of William*) I remember.
WILLIAM. We've just found him. He's Sir Gregory Upshott.
ANN (*moving to* R *of William*) That's right. Registered in the name of Charles Boughtflower.
LANDLORD. What name?
ANN. Boughtflower.
LANDLORD. I see.
WILLIAM. Incredible though it may seem, we believe that an attempt is going to be made here tonight to assassinate him.
LANDLORD. I see.
WILLIAM. As far as we can make out they've planted some kind of explosive somewhere on the premises, and we're expecting it to go up at ten forty-eight.
LANDLORD. I see.
WILLIAM. Don't keep saying "I see" like that. Can't you understand—everyone in the hotel's in mortal danger.
LANDLORD } (*together*) { I see!
WILLIAM } { I see! You've got to get everybody out of here—*now!*
LANDLORD (*deliberately*) I don't know how many you've had, but one thing I do know—you never had 'em here.
ANN. But it's going to go off.
WILLIAM. Look, let me put this in terms even you can understand—do you want to lose your pub?
LANDLORD. I don't want to lose my licence. I'm a broad-

minded man, but I'm not very partial to people who can't hold their liquor—especially if they bought it elsewhere.

(*The* LANDLORD *turns and exits up* C)

ANN (*wailing*) Now what are we going to do?
WILLIAM. Rouse the whole place while there's time.
ANN. How?
WILLIAM. Beat that gong. (*He runs to the gong* L, *picks up the stick and prepares to give the gong a good whack*)

(BOUGHTFLOWER *enters hurriedly down the stairs, carrying a suitcase*)

ANN (*seeing Boughtflower*) Bill—look! Get Sir Gregory to tell him.
WILLIAM (*replacing the gong stick and turning to Boughtflower*) Right. Listen, sir. You must talk to the landlord and make him understand that everyone else has got to clear out, too.
BOUGHTFLOWER. Eh?
WILLIAM. They're in danger as well—but of course you know that.
BOUGHTFLOWER. What's this?
WILLIAM. You've got to knock some sense into that landlord.
ANN. He refuses to believe you're Sir Gregory.
BOUGHTFLOWER. Sir which?
WILLIAM. Sir Gregory Upshott.
BOUGHTFLOWER. Who is?
WILLIAM }
ANN   } (*together*) You are.

(BOUGHTFLOWER *stares blankly at them*)

WILLIAM (*assailed by a horrible doubt*) Aren't you?
BOUGHTFLOWER. What d'you mean? I'm Charlie Boughtflower—always have been.
WILLIAM. My God, I believe he is.
BOUGHTFLOWER. Here—what's the game?
ANN. We thought you were Sir Gregory.
BOUGHTFLOWER. You mean you mistook me for Sir Gregory Upshott?
WILLIAM. Do you know him?
BOUGHTFLOWER. I've seen him once.
WILLIAM. Where?
BOUGHTFLOWER. At Newmarket, leading in his horse.
WILLIAM. Would you know him again?
BOUGHTFLOWER. No, he was the other side of the horse. (*He puts his suitcase on the floor up* LC) Here—what is all this, anyway?
WILLIAM. It's a matter of life and death. Please try to help. We think he's staying here.

BOUGHTFLOWER. If he is, I haven't seen him and I've seen most of 'em since I got here.
ANN. Oh, dear!
BOUGHTFLOWER. Wait a minute—I met a chap upstairs just now going into the—bathroom.
WILLIAM. What's he like?
BOUGHTFLOWER. I dunno—he was the other side of the door.
WILLIAM. Is he still up there?
BOUGHTFLOWER. I suppose so—only went in a couple of minutes ago.

(WILLIAM *promptly dashes for the stairs*)

(*Suddenly recollecting*) Here—where does my old woman come into this?
WILLIAM. She doesn't.
BOUGHTFLOWER. What?

(*The clock now stands at ten forty-seven.* ANN *looks at it and lets out a scream of alarm*)

ANN. The time! Look at the time!
WILLIAM (*looking at the clock*) My God! (*He takes a flying leap down the stairs*)
BOUGHTFLOWER (*bewildered*) Will somebody tell me what the hell's going on?
WILLIAM. There's something somewhere in this building that's going off at ten forty-eight.
BOUGHTFLOWER. Eh?
WILLIAM. It's intended for Upshott, most likely a bomb, but if we don't get out of here damned quick we'll all be blown to blazes.
BOUGHTFLOWER. Blimey O'Reilly!

(BOUGHTFLOWER *dashes out up* C)

WILLIAM. Oh, my God—look at the time—ten forty-eight. Under the table. Quick!

(ANN *and* WILLIAM *dive under the table* LC.
The LANDLORD *enters up* C. *He carries a tray with a bottle of champagne and two glasses. Seeing* WILLIAM *and* ANN *crouched under the table, he bolts for the door* L, *lest their obvious insanity should take a violent turn. He exits, and in his haste is heard to drop his tray with a crash in the dining-room*)

ANN (*emerging and getting to her feet*) Of course I did mention it might be the *Green Man*, Newhaven.
WILLIAM (*getting to his feet*) Nonsense! (*He crosses to the telephone and lifts the receiver. Into the telephone*) I want the *Green Man*, Newhaven. . . . Do you happen to know the number? . . . What? . . . Good—thank you . . . Will you connect me? (*He waits*)

ANN. There's scarcely any point in calling them up now, surely. Why not wait for the morning papers?
WILLIAM. It's ringing. (*Into the telephone*) Hullo? . . . Is that the *Green Man*, Newhaven? . . . Oh—er—are you still there? . . . You are? . . . Oh, well—er—good night. (*He replaces the receiver*) They're still there. Something's slipped.
ANN (*crossing to* RC) Things seem to have a habit of slipping with you.
WILLIAM (*moving to* L *of Ann*) You heard what that girl said. It was to go off at ten forty-eight.
ANN. You may remember I *did* suggest it might only be a figure of speech.
WILLIAM. Don't be ridiculous. How could a figure of speech endanger his life?
ANN. Well, then, we've come at the right time on the wrong day.
WILLIAM. What do you suggest—that we keep on coming down here until something—blows up?
ANN. I don't know why I let myself be talked into coming here in the first place.
WILLIAM. What! I suppose you think I arranged all this just to sell you a vacuum cleaner?
ANN. Nothing you did would surprise me.
WILLIAM (*complacently*) I admit I have a certain quality of unexpectedness. (*He coughs*) Unlike Reginald.
ANN. He phoned up just now.
WILLIAM. I know. I—er—caught the tail end of the conversation.
ANN (*quickly*) Did you?
WILLIAM. Yes. You gave me quite a nice build-up.
ANN. I think it's time we started back.
WILLIAM. Oh—wouldn't you like one for the road? I would.
ANN (*smiling*) All right.

(WILLIAM *moves to the hatch and raps on it. The hatch shutter opens and the* LANDLORD *peers out*)

WILLIAM. Can we have a drink?
LANDLORD. No. (*He slams down the shutter*)

(WILLIAM *raps on the shutter and the* LANDLORD *opens it*)

WILLIAM. Two to Charing Cross.
LANDLORD. Eh?
WILLIAMS. Could we have a couple of dry gingers?
LANDLORD (*astonished*) Dry gingers?
WILLIAM. Well, we'll have a dash of gin in them, if you absolutely insist. We are sadly changed characters, Landlord. Sober to a fault.
LANDLORD. No more funny business?

WILLIAM. No more funny business. Cross my heart.
LANDLORD. I'll—er—think about it. (*He closes the hatch*)
WILLIAM (*moving to L of Ann*) He'll—er—think about it.
ANN. What time will we get back to town, Mr Blake?
WILLIAM. About twelve-thirty, Miss Vincent. (*He pauses*) Tell me, how far have things gone with you and Reginald?
ANN. What do you mean?
WILLIAM. Anybody called any banns yet?
ANN. If you want to know, they have.
WILLIAM. Oh.
ANN (*after a slight pause*) Once.
WILLIAM (*brightening*) One up and two to play. Might be worse.
ANN. I can't see that it's anything to do with you.
WILLIAM. Can't you?
ANN. I only met you this evening.
WILLIAM. I know, but hasn't it been fun?
ANN. You've got a strange idea of fun. Besides, I don't go back on my word.
WILLIAM. You haven't given me the only reason that matters. Are you in love with him?
ANN. Why do you think I'm marrying him?
WILLIAM. I can't think of any really satisfactory reason. Can you honestly tell me that your heart beats any faster when he says, "Here is the forecast for shipping"?
ANN. What is all this leading up to?
WILLIAM. Me.
ANN. Don't be ridiculous! We've only known each other a couple of hours and we haven't agreed once.
WILLIAM. On what firmer basis could a marriage of two minds be built?

(*The* LANDLORD *enters up* C. *He carries a tray with two glasses of gin and two opened bottles of ginger ale*)

LANDLORD. Two gin and dry gingers. (*He puts the tray on the table* RC)
WILLIAM. You've come just in time.
LANDLORD. Eh? That'll be five shillings, please.
WILLIAM (*taking some coins from his pocket and handing them to the Landlord*) Keep the change.
LANDLORD. Thank you, sir. Mind if I turn the radio on? We like a bit of music on Saturday nights.

(WILLIAM *and* ANN *nod assent. The* LANDLORD *moves to the portable radio, switches it on then exits up* C)

ANN. What did you mean, he was just in time?
WILLIAM. Just too late.

(*The radio warms up and the* ANNOUNCER's *voice is heard. The clock now stands at ten fifty-two*)

ANNOUNCER. . . . Other parts were played by Hazel Warris, Percival Hermes, and Guy Hamilton. The play adapted for broadcasting by Edward Scaife and produced by Ernest Steward. The time is exactly ten forty-two.

(WILLIAM *reacts, nearly choking over his drink*)

The next part of the programme follows at ten forty-five.

(*The* LANDLORD *enters up* C)

WILLIAM. Landlord! That clock! Have you altered it?
LANDLORD. Of course. Put it on ten minutes.

(*The radio starts to play an interim record of the Chopin Waltz in A flat Major, Op. 69 No. 1*)

WILLIAM. My God!
ANN (*wailing*) We've still got six minutes to go.
WILLIAM. Six minutes! (*He makes a blind dash for the stairs*)

(*The* LANDLORD *stares dumbfounded*)

ANN. Where are you going?
WILLIAM. Upshott!
ANN. Where?
WILLIAM. First floor—in the bathroom.

(WILLIAM *exits up the stairs. The* LANDLORD *crosses deliberately to the table* RC, *picks up the tray of drinks and exits purposefully with them up* C. ANN *searches feverishly behind the window curtains for the bomb.*

LILY *enters up* C. *She carries a tray with two glasses of lager*)

LILY. Miss Vincent?
ANN. Yes?
LILY. He's on the phone again.
ANN. Who?
LILY. Your father. I've put you through.

(LILY *crosses and exits* L. ANN *moves impatiently to the telephone and lifts the receiver*)

ANN (*into the telephone; hurriedly*) Hullo? . . . Yes . . . Listen, Reginald—I can't talk now—there's no time . . . What? . . . No, I'll ring you back . . .

(HAWKINS *enters hurriedly* L. *He glances at Ann, then dismissing her as a casual customer, looks at his watch, then moves quickly to the radio and turns it up*)

(*Angrily*) No! I *can't* explain. Not now . . . There's no need to lose your temper . . . Well, why can't you wait till I get back? . . . All right, *break* it off. I'm sure it suits me. *Good*-bye. (*She replaces the receiver*)

HAWKINS (*crossing to* RC) Good evening.
ANN (*absently*) Good evening. (*She calls up the stairs*) Bill!

(ANN *looks with wild anxiety at the clock, then exits hurriedly up the stairs.*
      SIR GREGORY *and* JOAN *enter* L *and cross to* C. HAWKINS *watches them*)

SIR GREGORY. That cold rabbit pie was dreadful, diabolically dreadful. I must say, they manage these things differently in Irak. Why, there they think absolutely nothing of serving an entire sheep for the company. (*He looks at his watch and coughs*) Well, my dear, I rather think it's time we—er . . . (*He glances up the stairs*)
JOAN. Oh! Couldn't we have some coffee here first?
SIR GREGORY. We can have it sent up. In any event, it will certainly be foul. (*He takes* JOAN'S *arm and leads her towards the stairs*)
HAWKINS (*quickly interposing*) Perhaps you'd care to join me?
SIR GREGORY. Eh?
HAWKINS. I was just going to order some.
JOAN. Oh, thank goodness!
SIR GREGORY. Very kind of you, I'm sure, but under the circumstances . . . (*To* JOAN) Come along, my dear.
HAWKINS. In that case there's no point in my offering you a cigar.

(*The radio music ceases*)

SIR GREGORY. Not just now, thank you very much.

(SIR GREGORY *starts to lead the reluctant* JOAN *up the stairs.* HAWKINS *quickly takes a cigarette from his case and puts it in his mouth*)

HAWKINS. Oh. I wonder if I might trouble you for a light?
SIR GREGORY. Light? Of course. Here you are.

(SIR GREGORY *takes a box of matches from his pocket, drops it over the banisters to* HAWKINS *and exits with* JOAN *up the stairs*)

HAWKINS. Thank you. (*He lights his cigarette*)

(*The* ANNOUNCER *is heard on the radio*)

ANNOUNCER. This is the B.B.C. Home Service. The Middle East—a new approach. Here is a recording of the speech made today at a luncheon in the City by Sir Gregory Upshott, who has just been appointed Britain's Special Envoy.

(SIR GREGORY, *hearing his name, enters and comes down the stairs.* JOAN, *smiling with relief, follows him on*)

SIR GREGORY. Oh! (*He hesitates. To* JOAN) You run along, my dear, will you—I shan't be a moment.

(SIR GREGORY'S *speech comes from the radio and continues during*
E*

the ensuing dialogue. SIR GREGORY *sits on the chair* R *of the table* LC. JOAN *slips into the chair* L *of the table.* SIR GREGORY *glances at her, motioning her to go back up the stairs.* JOAN *shakes her head determinedly.* HAWKINS, *gratified, moves to the hall-stand, takes his overcoat from it and puts it on.*

WILLIAM *and* ANN *enter and come down the stairs.* HAWKINS *sees William, recognizes him, and abruptly turns his back*)

ANN. Are you sure it wasn't him?
WILLIAM (*crossing to* C) Positive.
ANN (*following William; quietly*) Isn't it time to beat that gong?

(HAWKINS *turns to the arch up* C)

WILLIAM (*glancing at the clock; uncertainly*) I don't know—wait a minute. (*He suddenly sees Hawkins, stares at him, then moves quickly to the arch up* C *and intercepts him*) What a very small world it is, to be sure.

(HAWKINS *is startled, but quickly recovers himself*)

HAWKINS. Are you addressing me, sir?
WILLIAM. What are you doing here—repairing clocks? Or looking for Sergeant Basset, perhaps?
HAWKINS. I don't think we've met.
WILLIAM (*to* Ann) This is your next door neighbour—"Windyridge".
HAWKINS. That does not happen to be my name.
WILLIAM (*taking Hawkins by the arm*) Take a look at the time.
HAWKINS. I can't recollect meeting either of you before. And yet your face is somehow familiar—(*he pulls himself free*) though not so odiously familiar as your manner.
WILLIAM. Do you know what the time is?
HAWKINS. Naturally. It is time to go. Good night.
WILLIAM (*taking the ancient revolver from his pocket*) Oh, no.
HAWKINS (*looking at the revolver*) Dear me, what's that?
WILLIAM. Your uncle's revolver, Mr Hawkins—but unlike him I'm not relying on the visual effect.
HAWKINS (*to* ANN) The man's as drunk as a lord or as mad as a hatter. I wonder which.
WILLIAM. You've got just over thirty seconds to tell us where you put it.
HAWKINS. Put what?

(SIR GREGORY, *struggling to hear his own radio speech, rises and moves very close to the radio receiver*)

LANDLORD (*off*) I tell you nothing's happened here. What d'you mean "blown up"?

(BOUGHTFLOWER *excitedly pushes the* LANDLORD *on up* C)

BOUGHTFLOWER. That's what he said.

LANDLORD. Who?
BOUGHTFLOWER (*pointing at* WILLIAM) Him! There he is. He's the one who told me.
LANDLORD. Oh—he did, did he?
BOUGHTFLOWER. You said the whole place was going up sky-high.
WILLIAM. So it is—in thirty seconds. (*To* HAWKINS) Isn't that so?
HAWKINS. The man's just drunk.

(SIR GREGORY, *unable to hear the speech, gives up the unequal contest and turns angrily on the others*)

SIR GREGORY. Can't you conduct your argument elsewhere? The place is a bedlam and I am trying to listen to an important broadcast. Thank you.

(ANN *sees the clock, which is practically on ten fifty-eight. She lets out a cry*)

ANN. Bill—the time!

(HAWKINS *sees his chance and dives out up* C)

RADIO. "... the moment of impact may not be far ahead ..."
WILLIAM. Listen! (*He looks from the radio to Sir Gregory, then back to the radio*)
RADIO. "... If I can help to bring about a new settlement ..."
SIR GREGORY (*clearing his throat*) Hrrm!

(*The voice on the radio does the same immediately afterwards*)

WILLIAM. Good God! Then you're Sir Gregory. That's your voice. It must be in the radio. Look out, everybody! (*He rushes forward, seizes the radio, dashes with it to the french windows and hurls it out over the balcony*)

(*The voice of* SIR GREGORY *continues from the radio*)

RADIO. "... I shall then indeed feel that my task will be done and I will be able to disappear, this time finally, from the public scene."

(JOAN *rises and runs with* SIR GREGORY, *the* LANDLORD, ANN *and* BOUGHTFLOWER *to the window. A violent explosion is heard off, followed by a rumbling as of falling sections of cliff.*
LILY *enters* L)

SIR GREGORY. Good heavens!
LILY (*crossing to* C) What on earth was that?
LANDLORD. Only half the cliff being blown away. Pop upstairs and tell everyone it's all right, no bones broken.
LILY. O.K.

(LILY *exits up the stairs*.
  The LANDLORD *exits up* C. WILLIAM *comes in from the balcony*)

WILLIAM. Where's that fellow gone?

(*The sound of a car driving off is heard*)

There goes his car. (*To Boughtflower*) Get after him in yours—I'll phone the police.

(BOUGHTFLOWER *exits hurriedly up* C. WILLIAM *crosses to the telephone, but is checked by* SIR GREGORY)

SIR GREGORY. Pardon me, sir, but you seem to know something about this.

WILLIAM. Up to a point, yes.

SIR GREGORY (*crossing to* C) What was that explosion?

(JOAN *and* ANN *stand down* RC)

WILLIAM (*moving to* L *of Sir Gregory*) An attempt on your life, Sir Gregory.

SIR GREGORY. What?

JOAN (*wailing*) He knows who you are. I'm not staying here now, I'm *not*, Sir Gregory.

SIR GREGORY. Be quiet. And *do* sit down. (*To William*) Just a minute. You mean to say that in that radio there was an explosive?

WILLIAM. Certainly.

SIR GREGORY. Who put it there?

WILLIAM. The man who just went out. Answers to the name of Hawkins.

SIR GREGORY. I don't know the name.

WILLIAM. It's unlikely to be his real one.

SIR GREGORY. I see. Well—why are we waiting? Telephone the police. Tell them who I am, and . . .

WILLIAM. Is that advisable, sir?

JOAN. Oh, no, no—of course it's not.

SIR GREGORY. That is for me to say.

WILLIAM. Naturally, but I didn't think you'd want to give evidence in court—with the young lady. I mean, think of the newspapers, sir.

JOAN (*wailing*) And mother takes the *Daily Mirror*.

SIR GREGORY. She would.

WILLIAM. Why not leave here now, sir? I'll have to make a statement after you've gone, but if you move out now there'll be no proof you've ever been here. After all, no harm's been done—in any direction.

SIR GREGORY. Perhaps you're right. (*To Joan*) We'll leave at once.

JOAN. Oh, thank you, sir. (*She moves to the fireplace, looks in the mirror over the mantelpiece and tidies herself*)

SIR GREGORY (*to William; in an undertone*) You're M.I.Five, I take it.
WILLIAM. No, sir. Nothing so glamorous.
SIR GREGORY. Oh. Then what are you?
WILLIAM. I—er—well, you might say I just go about cleaning up things. Blake's the name, sir. I represent the Electro-Broom, the Little Wizard of the Carpet. (*He hands Sir Gregory his card*) My card, sir.
SIR GREGORY. H'm? All I can say is, I owe you a great deal, a very great deal.
WILLIAM (*recovering his card*) Pardon me, sir. It's the only one I've got.
SIR GREGORY. H'rrm. Yes. (*To Joan*) Are you ready, my dear?
JOAN (*brightly*) Oh, yes, I'm *waiting*.
SIR GREGORY (*to William*) I'll see you get recognition for this.
WILLIAM. Thank you, sir. I hope you avoid it.
SIR GREGORY. I . . . Hrrm! Good night.
WILLIAM }
ANN } (*together*) { Good night, sir.
{ Good night.

(SIR GREGORY *and* JOAN *exit up* C)

WILLIAM. Another couple of minutes and I'd have sold him an Electro-Broom.

(*The* LANDLORD *enters up* C. *He carries a tray with two glasses of champagne*)

LANDLORD (*crossing and putting the tray on the table* LC) I want to thank you two. I've got to take back everything I said.
ANN (*to William*) Perhaps you could sell *him* one.
LANDLORD. I've just been out and had a look at the cliff. If that thing had gone up in here there wouldn't have been a bottle left in the place.
WILLIAM. I'm sorry about your radio, Landlord.
LANDLORD. That's all right, sir. The old one still works. (*He moves to the radiogram, switches it on, then points to the champagne and smiles*) That's on the house, sir.

(*The* LANDLORD *exits up* C. *The radio warms up and the music of Borodin's Nocturne for String Orchestra is heard*)

WILLIAM. Worried about something?
ANN. I'm feeling a bit limp after all that excitement.
WILLIAM. Ah, yes. (*He sighs*) The purple patch has faded. Back to the humdrum—and Reginald.
ANN. I didn't tell you—he made another toll-call.
WILLIAM. Don't worry—he's sure to charge it to expenses.
ANN. He's broken it off.
WILLIAM. What? Oh. That makes a difference—or doesn't it?
ANN. I don't know. Perhaps he didn't mean it.

WILLIAM. You ought to have snapped up an offer like that.
ANN. I don't know what to do.
WILLIAM. You might consider me.
ANN (*looking at him*) Do you think so? Why?
WILLIAM. I need companionship. I couldn't face the future throwing bombs out of windows all alone. It *was* fun, wasn't it?

(*The music ceases*)

ANN. Mmm.
WILLIAM. Ann!

(WILLIAM *is about to embrace Ann when the* RADIO ANNOUNCER *is heard*)

ANNOUNCER. This is the B.B.C. Third Programme.
WILLIAM (*interjecting*) We could do without that.
ANNOUNCER. Five minutes of Free Verse.
WILLIAM (*interjecting*) Ann, what I wanted . . .
ANNOUNCER. Here is Reginald Willoughby-Pratt, who will read a group of poems by Milton Boyle, to which the author has given the title *Vicious Cycle*. Reginald Willoughby-Pratt.

(ANN *and* WILLIAM *look quickly at each other*. REGINALD'S *voice is now heard. It shows the effects of strain, a strain which increases*)

REGINALD. "Her beauty has a kind of ugliness,
    A strangulating loveliness,
    Compressing the jugular of my sensitivity
    As ivy constricts trunk of tree,

(WILLIAM *crosses to the window seat and picks up Ann's coat*)

    Turning aboreal royalty
    Into beanpole servitors,

(WILLIAM *crosses to* ANN *and helps her on with her coat*)

    Burying the berries
    In a fruitless operation—
    So that the name of her,
    Ann—

(*His voice falters at this unfortunate coincidence*)

(WILLIAM *and* ANN *are checked at the mention of the name*)

    Asininely monosyllabic,
    The mere label she goes by
    Yet pulsing with drum beat—
    Ann—Ann—Ann—Ann . . ."

(WILLIAM *and* ANN *are again arrested as they make for the arch up* C)

(*His voice cracks under the altogether intolerable strain, this is too much, much too much. His voices takes on another, completely human note*) Ann! I can't go on. I won't. Listen to me, Ann, wherever you are. You can go to your bloody vacuum cleaner! I'm through—you . . .

(*He is switched off abruptly with an extra definite click.* WILLIAM *and* ANN *look at each other in amazement. The* ANNOUNCER'S *voice is heard on the radio*)

ANNOUNCER. We must apologize to listeners for a technical hitch. And that brings us to the end of today's broadcasting in the Third Programme. Good night, everyone.

WILLIAM } (*together*) Good night.
ANN

ANNOUNCER. *Good* night.

ANN *and* WILLIAM *exit up* C *as—*

the CURTAIN *falls*

SIR GREGORY UPSHOTT'S SPEECH

Mr Chairman, my lords, ladies and gentlemen. Hrrm! I have always liked to think that I am fundamentally a modest man, but after your extremely flattering remarks, Mr Chairman, I confess I am finding the part somewhat difficult to sustain.

(*There is a ripple of polite laughter*)

Were I the walking compendium of all the commercial and diplomatic talents that he has described I would certainly be priceless indeed.

(*There is laughter*)

But I am afraid—I am very much afraid—that I am not. Nevertheless, I think I can promise that such ability as I may have will be unremittingly devoted to the task to which I have been appointed.

I have spent, I suppose, the best years of my life in the Middle East and at one time entertained serious thoughts of embracing the Moslem faith. As a youthful orientalist I studied the civilization of ancient Egypt, and in later years I served under our Minister in Cairo. I have hunted with the Kings of Irak and shot with the Shahs of Iran. I watched the birth pangs of the new Palestine with a friendly eye and studied the obscurer dialects of Syria.

What do we find in those regions of today? A vital area for British Commonwealth interests, a variety of resources, strategic bases of stupendous importance, and, at the same time, diverse peoples, poverty, backwardness, pressures and frictions, age-long enmities, distrust and suspicion.

What is really wanted is a new deal. If our friends in those parts could look upon themselves and ourselves with a fresh eye and so bury the past—what is there that could not be done?

(*There is applause and cries of "Hear, hear"*)

The Egyptian fellaheen must learn to lie down with the Israeli. Ourselves and the Americans must make an entirely new approach in Iran. Oil is, I confess, much in my mind—it has to be. The future of our military bases must come into it, too.

The international situation makes every aspect of my task urgent. Indeed, elements in certain countries that shall be nameless have threatened, openly and covertly, to take any steps that may be necessary to ensure that my mission shall be a failure. *Any* steps, gentlemen—that is what we have come to. For myself, I remain quite unintimidated——

(*There is a murmur of applause*)

—indeed I am greatly encouraged, because such threats would never be made unless they feared that my mission might be successful.

It is a platitude, but a true one, to say to our friends in that part of the globe that we must hang together or hang separately. In the common interest we must all unite. The moment of impact may not be so far ahead. If I can help to bring about a new settlement—hrrm!—I shall then indeed feel that my task will be done, and I will be able to disappear, this time finally, from the public scene.

FURNITURE AND PROPERTY PLOT

PROLOGUE

On stage: Table. *On it:* desk lamp, microphone, typescript
           Chair
           Waste-paper basket

ACT I

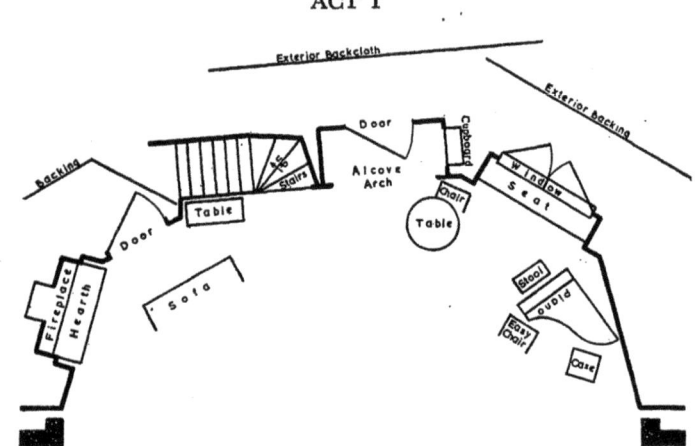

On stage: Sofa. *On it:* dust sheet, 2 cushions
              Under it: lady's red umbrella
           Easy chair. *On it:* dust sheet
           Circular table. *On it:* dust sheet, ashtray
           Upright chair
           Occasional table. *On it:* 2 tumblers, wine glass, syphon of soda,
              bottle of whisky
                      Under it: folded dust sheet
           *Grand piano. *On it:* dust sheet
           Piano stool
           Window seat. *On it:* 3 cushions, 4 framed pictures, telephone
              concealed behind upstage window curtain
           Pair net curtains
           Pair chintz curtains
           Pelmet

                    * See note on page 77.

Carpet on floor
3 rugs
Stair carpet
On mantelpiece: ashtray, packet of cigarettes, box of matches
Over mantelpiece: 2 pairs electric-candle wall-brackets
On skirting above fireplace: 15 amp power point
Packing case. *In it:* books, A.A. handbook, length of picture cord
　　　　　　　On it: modern wall mirror
On floor down L: 5 framed pictures
Light switches on R wall of alcove C
In cupboard L *of alcove:* mop, set to fall out
On front door: Yale lock, letter-box, both practical
Over exterior of front door: name-plate "Appleby"
Outside front door: door mat
In front garden: border with tulips and foliage

Set:　*On floor below sofa:* cushion
　　　On floor above easy chair (concealed): towel with red stains
Window curtains closed
Windows open
Front door closed
Door R open
Upright chair on side
Corner of rug LC turned back
　　　On table LC: Montague's jacket
　　　　　　　　　Montague's bowler hat lined with newspaper

Off stage: Towel (MONTAGUE)
　　　　　Wooden box with handle. *In it:* body of vacuum cleaner with flex plugged in, suction tube, 2 metal extension tubes, 4 nozzle attachments, Airwick bottle with spray, instruction pamphlet, bag of silver sand, bag of soot (WILLIAM)
　　　　　Parcel (ANN)
　　　　　Modiste's box. *In it:* housecoat, foundation garment (ANN)
　　　　　Dustpan, brush (WILLIAM)
　　　　　Framed picture (Mill House and Pool) wrapped in green baize and tied with picture cord (REGINALD)
　　　　　2 parcels (REGINALD)
　　　　　Large envelope. *In it:* poem (REGINALD)
　　　　　Bowler hat and umbrella (REGINALD)

Personal: WILLIAM: business card, packet of cigarettes, matches, handkerchief
　　　　　Ann: handbag. *In it:* Yale key
　　　　　REGINALD: Yale key, watch

ACT II

Scene 1

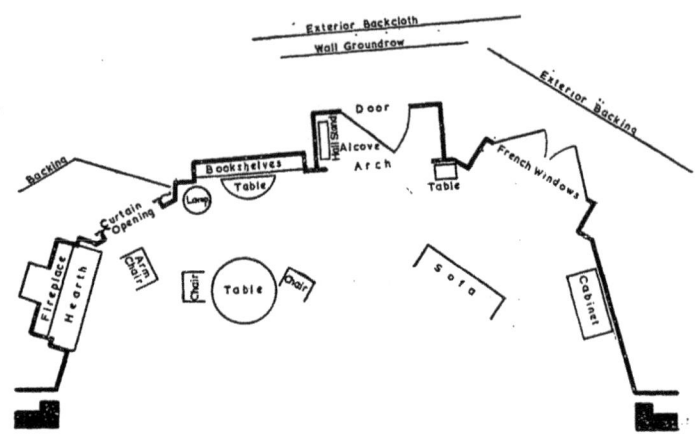

On stage: Sofa. *On it:* 2 cushions
    Circular table (RC) *On it:* chess board and men, box with cigarettes, ashtray, matches
    2 upright chairs
    Armchair. *On it:* cushion
    Console table. *On it:* tape recorder
        In drawer: loaded pistol
    Built-in bookshelves. *On them:* books
    Cabinet (down L) *On it:* syphon of soda in holder, jar with tobacco, silverware, bottle of whisky, bottle of sherry, bottle of gin, tumbler, whisky glass, ashtray, table lamp
    Hall-stand. *On it:* Hawkins' overcoat, sergeant's helmet with bicycle clips inside
        On shelf: attache-case with pliers, screwdriver, detonator, Hawkins' hat
    Standard lamp
    Net curtains at window
    Heavy curtains and pelmet at window
    Occasional table. *On it:* telephone with loose flex and plug
    Pictures on walls
    Over mantelpiece: 2 pairs electric-candle wall-brackets
    On mantelpiece: china and ormolu clock, pair of candelabra, ashtray

MEET A BODY

        In hearth: electric fire, companion set
        Carpet on floor
        Hearthrug
        Rug (*up* c)
        Outside front door: name-plate "Windyridge", door mat
        In front garden: hedge border
Window curtains open
Windows closed
Front door closed
Door R open

Off stage: Dust sheet MONTAGUE

Personal: HAWKINS: pipe, stop-watch

SCENE 2

Setting exactly as at the end of Act I
Check: On *sofa:* name-plate, poem in envelope, lady's umbrella, bowler hat
        On *window seat:* Ann's two boxes open, containing wrap and foundation garment
        On *piano:* green baize and cord
        In hearth: dustpan and brush
        Leaning against window seat: picture

Strike: Dust sheet from under table RC
Window open
Window curtains open
Front door open
Door R open

Off stage: Revolver (MONTAGUE)
        Chloroform pad (MONTAGUE)

ACT III

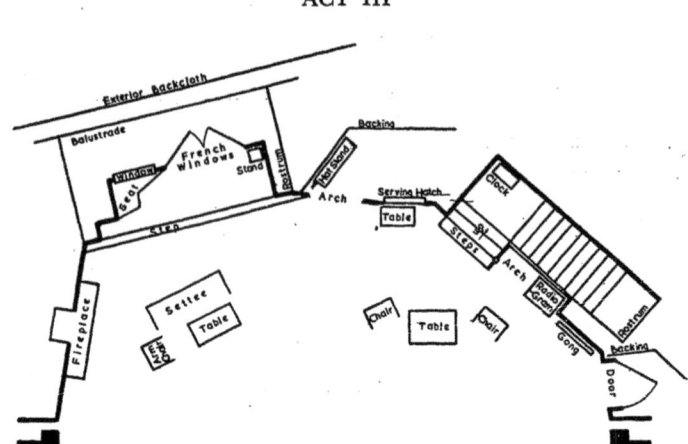

On stage: Wicker settee
2 wicker tables
Wicker armchair
2 upright wicker chairs
Radiogram. *On it:* small white portable radio receiver
Large gong with stand and beater
Grandfather clock (practical)
Small table (up c) *On it:* telephone, ashtray, advertisement
Tall stand with aspidistra
Hall-stand. *On it:* hotel register, hats and coats
Carpet on floor
Rugs
Fender
Fire-irons
Basket grate
On mantelpiece: ornaments, advertisements, ashtray, 2 glass mats, 2 used glasses
Over mantelpiece: mirror, glass case with stuffed fish, 2 swan-neck electric brackets
Window curtains and pelmet
Sporting prints on walls
Carpet on stairs
Over stairs: swan-neck electric bracket
Framed menu
Advertisements
Window seat. *On it:* cushions
On hatch shelf: rubber mats, advertisement

    Over door L: swan-neck electric bracket
    Bell push above fireplace

Set: *On table* RC: ashtray, glass mat, glass of whisky, *Evening News,* football pool coupons
   Under it: magazines
   On table LC: ashtray, 2 glass mats, 2 used glasses
   Under it: magazines
   Below hatch: Boughtflower's suitcase
French windows open
Door L closed
Lights on

Off stage: Attaché-case. *In it:* flex, pliers, screwdriver (HAWKINS)
    Plant in pot (LANDLORD)
    Suitcase (BOUGHTFLOWER)
    Tray. *On it:* bottle of champagne, 2 champagne glasses (LANDLORD)
    Tray. *On it:* 2 glasses of gin, 2 opened bottles of ginger ale (LANDLORD)
    Tray. *On it:* 2 glasses of lager (LILY)
    Tray. *On it:* 2 glasses of champagne (LANDLORD)

Personal: HAWKINS: watch
      overcoat. *In pocket:* bottle of tablets, case with cigarettes
    JOAN: handbag. *In it:* handkerchief
    LILY: watch
    BOUGHTFLOWER: cigar, box of matches
    LANDLORD: watch
    WILLIAM: coins, revolver, business card
    SIR GREGORY: watch, box of matches

  In the London production an empty piano case was used. The frame had been removed and the side nearest the wall cut away. A corresponding cut was made in the scenery, and the actress playing Winifred took up her position inside the piano only a few moments before the lid was opened. As such a piano will not be readily obtainable a dummy arm has been made by Messrs Charles H. Fox Ltd, 184 High Holborn, London, W.C.1, which can be fitted into any ordinary piano.

LIGHTING PLOT

Property fittings required:
        Desk lamp (practical)
        2 pairs electric-candle wall-brackets (not practical)
        2 pairs electric-candle wall-brackets (practical)
        Standard lamp (practical)
        4 swan-neck wall-brackets (practical)
        Tape recorder (practical)
        Radiogram
        Portable radio
        Vacuum cleaner
        1 15 amp power point
        Light switch

PROLOGUE

A cameo set C in front of TABS
THE APPARENT SOURCE OF LIGHT is a desk lamp C

To open: A small spotlight in the footlights focused on to REGINALD seated at the table down C
Desk lamp lit

Cue 1   REGINALD: ... into the film business   (page 1)
Quick dim of spot to BLACK-OUT
Snap out desk lamp

ACT I

Interior. Early on a May evening
THE MAIN ACTING AREAS are at the sofa (RC) and below the table (LC)
THE APPARENT SOURCE OF LIGHT is a large casement window L

To open: Bright sunlight outside window L and front door C
White and amber strip outside door R
On-stage lights checked to $\frac{1}{2}$

Cue 2   MONTAGUE opens window curtain   (page 2)
Bring up on-stage lights to full

ACT II, SCENE 1

Interior. A May evening
THE MAIN ACTING AREAS are at the sofa (LC) and at a small table (RC)
THE APPARENT SOURCES OF LIGHT are: in daytime, french windows L and at night, a standard lamp up RC, a table lamp L and 2 pairs electric-candle wall-brackets over the fireplace R

To open:	Sunset effect outside window L and front door C	
	White and amber strip outside door R	
	On-stage lights checked to ¾	
Cue 3	HAWKINS closed window curtains	(page 26)
	Check on-stage lights to ¼	
Cue 4	HAWKINS switches on lights	(page 26)
	Bring up on-stage lights to full and snap in standard lamp, table lamp and wall-brackets	
Cue 5	MONTAGUE switches off lights	(page 30)
	Check on-stage lights to ¼ and snap out standard lamp, table lamp and wall-brackets	

ACT I, SCENE 2
    Setting as Act I
To open: Lights as at the end of Act I
Cue 6   *During the scene the lights dim a little as night begins to fall*

ACT III
    Interior. Night
    THE MAIN ACTING AREAS are at a settee (RC) a table (LC) and a radiogram (up LC)
    THE APPARENT SOURCES OF LIGHT are electric wall-brackets, two over the fireplace R, one L and one on a staircase up LC
To open: Blue outside window with distant effect on backcloth of pier lights
    Brackets lit
    On-stage lights full up
No Cues

EFFECTS PLOT

ACT I

Cue 1	MONTAGUE picks up overturned chair Church clock in distance chimes ½ hour	(page 2)

ACT II

SCENE 1

Cue 2	SERGEANT: Take your time Mantelpiece clock chimes seven	(page 21)
Cue 3	HAWKINS starts tape recorder Sir Gregory's speech	(page 29)
Cue 4	HAWKINS exits Sound of car departing	(page 30)

SCENE 2

No Cues

ACT III

Cue 5	HAWKINS switches on the radio Dance music	(page 51)
Cue 6	HAWKINS switches off the radio Dance music ceases	(page 51)
Cue 7	WILLIAM opens clock Clock strikes ½ hour	(page 54)
Cue 8	LANDLORD: Put it on ten minutes Radio music. Record of the Chopin Waltz in A Flat Major, Op. 69, No. 1	(page 62)
Cue 9	HAWKINS: . . . you a cigar Music ceases	(page 63)
Cue 10	SIR GREGORY: I shan't be a moment Sir Gregory's speech	(page 63)
Cue 11	Three seconds after radio is flung out of window Explosion and noise of cliff falling	(page 65)
Cue 12	WILLIAM: Where's that fellow gone? Sound of car departing	(page 66)
Cue 13	LANDLORD: That's on the house, sir Radio music. Borodin's Nocturne for String Orchestra	(page 67)
Cue 14	WILLIAM: It was fun, wasn't it? Fade radio music	(page 68)